SIGNING THEIR LIVES AWAY

ALSO BY THE AUTHORS

Signing Their Rights Away
Stuff Every American Should Know

ALSO BY DENISE KIERNAN

The Girls of Atomic City
The Last Castle

SIGNING THEIR LIVES AWAY

THE FAME AND MISFORTUNE
OF THE MEN WHO SIGNED
The Declaration of Independence

BY DENISE KIERNAN & JOSEPH D'AGNESE

Library of Congress Cataloging in Publication Number: 2018961372

ISBN: 978-1-68369-126-6

Printed in Canada
Typeset in Adobe Garamond Pro, Brandon Grotesque, and Australis Pro Swash
Designed by Aurora Parlagreco
Production management by John J. McGurk

Photo credits: Imagery from "Portraits and Autographs of the Signers of the Declaration of Independence," lithograph by Ole Erekson, ca. 1876. Courtesy of the Library of Congress, Washington DC.

Quirk Books
215 Church Street
Philadelphia, PA 19106
quirkbooks.com

10 9 8 7 6 5 4 3

CONTENTS

XI. NORTH CAROLINA

XII. SOUTH CAROLINA

XIII. GEORGIA

APPENDIXES

INTRODUCTION

In 1776, fifty-six men risked their lives to defy the British and sign their names to the Declaration of Independence, but most Americans can't name more than a handful.

There's John Hancock, of course. And most people will correctly identify Thomas Jefferson, Benjamin Franklin, and John Adams. But then the guessing begins: George Washington? Paul Revere? Thomas Paine?

The Declaration of Independence is America's birth certificate, its most celebrated document, and a model for later declarations crafted by struggling peoples the world over. Its signers were men who drew upon the best within themselves in the face of horrifyingly difficult circumstances.

They also lived remarkably interesting lives. True, most of them were privileged members of the elite upper classes, but quite a few were just the opposite. And all these men were impacted by death, suffering, and adversity. Many were orphaned; even more lost children and wives for no other reason than that, in those days, the flu was deadly. So was asthma. So was a bad bout of diarrhea. Yet all these men carried on.

Over the years, we've read newspaper articles and junk e-mails seeking to quantify and magnify the sufferings of the signers. Every July, their miseries are dusted off and trotted out along with barbecues and flags. It's a shame that this is the only time of year Americans think about these men. But it's even more disheartening to discover that most of the stories are just plain false.

In the end, it doesn't matter that none of the signers were killed for affixing their name to the Declaration of Independence or that none died in battle. What does matter is that they came together one sweltering summer under distressing circumstances and, despite huge differences in opinion, backgrounds, and values, decided to band together and form a new nation. Doing so was, without a doubt, an enormous, life-threatening risk, and if the colonies had not been triumphant—and honestly, it's astounding that they were—these men would have surely been, as they used to say back in the day, fitted with a "halter."

As the Declaration of Independence so eloquently states in its last line, they risked their lives, their fortunes, and their sacred honor.

We think they are worth knowing.

A Clarification: The Real Independence Day

Happy Fourth of July! Wait, scratch that. We mean: Happy Second of July! Hold on, that's still not right: Happy Second of August!

John Adams thought that future generations of Americans should celebrate Independence Day "with Pomp and Parade, with Shows, Games, Sports, Guns, Bells, Bonfires and Illuminations from one End of this Continent to the other from this Time forward forever more." Adams omitted the burgers, hot dogs, and beer kegs, but his heart was in the right place. Oddly, when he wrote these words to his wife, Abigail, on July 3, 1776, he wasn't talking about the Fourth of July. He was speaking of what he considered to be the nation's true birthday: July 2, 1776.

The events leading up to that date were as follows: On June 7, 1776, Richard Henry Lee of Virginia proposed that the colonies break with England. Though the citizenry had debated this point for years, the thought of finally doing the deed shook the delegates. To calm themselves, they did what any political body would do: they postponed the vote for a month. During that time, a committee of five congressmen—Thomas Jefferson, Benjamin Franklin, John Adams, Robert R. Livingston, and Roger Sherman—was appointed to write the Declaration of Independence. Jefferson ended up doing most of the heavy lifting, with some editorial suggestions from Adams and Franklin.

Tensions were running high by July 1, the day of an "unofficial" vote. Only nine colonies supported the break. South Carolina and Pennsylvania voted no, Delaware was deadlocked, and New York abstained. But when the official vote came on July 2, twelve of the thirteen colonies voted in favor. New York abstained again; they were waiting for permission that was held up in Ye Olde Trafficke but promised they would likely vote yea in a few days. It wasn't exactly unanimous, but Congress went with it anyway. The motion carried. A new nation was born.

For the next two days, Congress polished the language of the Declaration, and the document was officially adopted on July 4. But only two men—President of Congress John Hancock and his secretary, Charles Thomson—actually signed the document on that day. Shortly after, a local printer named John Dunlap set the words into type, and about 200 copies were distributed throughout the new thirteen states. When Americans saw the July 4 date emblazoned at the top of Dunlap's broadside, they mistook the date of adoption for the day of the momentous vote. In fact, it wasn't until August 2, 1776, that the majority of the signers affixed their signatures to a fancier version of the "unanimous" Declaration—the one displayed today at the National Archives in Washington, D.C.

By August 1776, thousands of colonists were already regarding July 4 as the most important date in their fledgling nation's history. To avoid upsetting this pleasant fiction, Congress sneakily backdated some official records to show that all fifty-six men had signed on July 4, 1776. Of course, this introduced a bizarre anachronism into the final record: the men who were present in Philadelphia and who voted for independence on July 2 were not the same group of men who signed on August 2! By the time

August 2 rolled around, some of the original voters were out of town, fighting in the war, helping their states write new constitutions—or they had been replaced by entirely new delegates. Moreover, not all the delegates could make it to the big affair on August 2, and so they signed when they could get around to it—one as late as 1781.

But that doesn't make for a tidy story, does it? No wonder Americans have wished one another a Happy Fourth of July ever since.

S, JULY 4, 1776.

united States of America.

ple to dissolve the political bands which have connected them with another, and to
God entitle them, a decent respect to the opinions of mankind requires that they
self-evident, that all men are created equal, that they are endowed by their Creator
to secure these rights, Governments are instituted among Men, deriving their just
ends, it is the Right of the People to alter or to abolish it, and to institute new
hall seem most likely to effect their Safety and Happiness. Prudence, indeed,
dingly all experience hath shewn, that mankind are more disposed to suffer, while
in along train of abuses and usurpations, pursuing invariably the same Object
overnment, and to provide new Guards for their future security — Such has
ormer Systems of Government. The history of the present King of Great
lute Tyranny over these States. To prove this, let Facts be submitted to a candid
good. ——— He has forbidden his Governors to pass Laws of immediate
suspended, he has utterly neglected to attend to them ——— He has refused to
Representation in the Legislature, a right inestimable to them and formidable
from the depository of their Public Records, for the sole purpose of fatiguing them into
ranly firmness his invasions on the rights of the people ——— He has refused for
uhilation, have returned to the People at large for their exercise; the State remain
has endeavoured to prevent the Population of these States; for that purpose obstruc-
ing the conditions of new Appropriations of Lands. ——— He has obstructed the
ade Judges dependent on his Will alone, for the tenure of their offices, and the amount
fficers to harass our People, and eat out their substance ——— He has kept among
Military independent of and superior to the Civil power ——— He has combined
is Assent to their Acts of pretended Legislation: ——— For Quartering large bodies of
they should commit on the Inhabitants of these States: ——— For cutting off
us in many cases, of the benefits of Trial by Jury; ——— For transporting us beyond
Province, establishing therein an Arbitrary government, and enlarging its Boundaries
ies: ——— For taking away our Charters, abolishing our most valuable Laws, and
ing themselves invested with powers to legislate for us in all cases whatsoever. ——
He has plundered our seas, ravaged our Coasts, burnt our towns, and destroyed the lives
th, desolation and tyranny, already begun with circumstances of Cruelty & perfidy
onstrained our fellow Citizens taken Captive on the high Seas to bear Arms against

I.

New Hampshire

Josiah Bartlett

THE SIGNER IMMORTALIZED ON *THE WEST WING*

BORN: November 21, 1729

DIED: May 19, 1795

AGE AT SIGNING: 46

PROFESSION: Physician

BURIED: Plains Cemetery, Kingston, New Hampshire

Live Free or Die" is one of the least-subtle state mottos in the United States, and the signers from New Hampshire, especially Josiah Bartlett, led lives that do justice to this phrase.

Bartlett came from a humble background. As the son of a cobbler, he lacked access to formal education, so he studied medicine with a local doctor (a custom at the time) and eventually began a successful practice in Kingston, New Hampshire. Despite his revolutionary political leanings, the royal government favored him—for a while. His political career started around 1765 when he became a member of New Hampshire's provincial assembly and received appointments from the governor as a colonel in the militia and as a justice of the peace. He was stripped of these titles as his involvement in the cause of independence became more high-profile, but this didn't hinder his work. When the governor disbanded the provincial assembly, Bartlett and other like-minded patriots formed the New Hampshire Provincial Congress instead.

Bartlett is often included on the list of those signers who had their homes burned by the British because they signed the Declaration, but that isn't exactly true. Bartlett was elected to the First Continental Congress in 1774 but couldn't attend because his house had burned to the ground. This information suggests that the house was destroyed long before he ever signed the Declaration.

Bartlett was the first man to cast a vote for independence on July 2, the first to approve the Declaration on July 4, and the first—after the president of the Continental Congress, John Hancock—to sign the engrossed "final draft" of the document on August 2. New Hampshire boosters often imply that their state was first in all Congressional matters because New Hampshire was such an enthusiastic supporter of independence. In actuality, Congress proceeded in geographical order, starting in the north and working its way south along the eastern seaboard. (We elected to follow this same order when organizing this book.)

After signing the Declaration of Independence, Bartlett lent his medical skills to the New Hampshire militia and the Continental troops when they took on General John Burgoyne at Bennington, New York. (The hero of that battle, General John Stark, is credited with coining the phrase "Live Free or Die.") In 1778, when it came time for Congress to vote on the Articles of Confederation, Bartlett was back, and once again he was first in line. Then he left Congress to be with his wife and kids.

Bartlett's return to New Hampshire did not take him out of politics entirely. The doctor with no formal medical—or legal—training was soon the chief justice of the New Hampshire court of common pleas and eventually chief justice of the superior court. Bartlett also played a major role leading New Hampshire to ratify the Constitution. This was particularly significant because, as stated in Article VII, "The Ratification of the Conventions of nine States shall be sufficient for the Establishment of this Constitution between the States so ratifying the Same." New Hampshire was the ninth state to ratify the Constitution, and it therefore put the document officially into play for the new nation. After the deed was done, Bartlett was elected the state's first senator. He declined the position but went on to serve as president of New Hampshire. Then, when "president" was changed to "governor," he was the first to bear that title, too.

Though his political responsibilities often kept him from medicine, he never abandoned his calling. In 1790, Dartmouth College awarded him an honorary doctor of medicine degree, and Bartlett was a founder and first president of the New Hampshire Medical Society. Three of his sons and seven of his grandsons also became doctors. The patriarch of this supremely medical family ended up resigning the governorship because of poor health. He was sixty-five years old when he died in 1795, but his legacy survives in countless reruns of *The West Wing*. (The president played by Martin Sheen had almost the exact same name—Josiah Bartlet.)

Josiah Bartlett

William Whipple

THE SIGNER WHO FOUGHT FOR FREEDOM—WITH HIS SLAVE

BORN: January 14, 1730

DIED: November 28, 1785

AGE AT SIGNING: 46

PROFESSION: Sea captain, merchant, general

BURIED: North Cemetery, Portsmouth, New Hampshire

As a boy, Maine-born William Whipple went to sea and was so able-bodied that he attained the rank of ship's captain by the age of twenty-one. His travels took him to Africa, the West Indies, and Europe. These destinations offer a clue about the type of boat Whipple was sailing: he was, at least for a time, a slave trader. He not only profited from the business but also kept some slaves of his own, including an enslaved African named Prince who fought beside him during the Revolutionary War.

The details of his slaving days are sketchy, but they must have been highly lucrative. While some signers struggled their whole lives to sock away enough money to survive (William Ellery and Button Gwinnett, we're looking at you), Whipple appears to have made his fortune early. He amassed such wealth that he was able to retire forever from the sea in 1759. He then joined his brothers in the mercantile business but eventually retired by 1775, when he was only forty-five years old. Like the frugal-minded Benjamin Franklin, who retired from business at age forty-two, Whipple decided to devote himself to public service.

In 1775, Whipple and his compatriot General John Stark were named commanders of the New Hampshire militia. Whipple headed the first brigade, Stark the second. In January 1776—more than six months before the famous vote in Congress—New Hampshire became the first colony to declare independence from the king. Whipple was among the first men who helped form the new government there. Shortly thereafter, he was sent to Philadelphia to serve on the Continental Congress.

Whipple and fellow New Hampshire signer Josiah Bartlett voted for the Lee Resolution on July 2. (New Hampshire's third signer, Matthew Thornton, did not join Congress until September 1776.) Because Congressional protocol called for votes to be submitted in order from northernmost colony to southernmost, Bartlett and Whipple cast the first votes for independence and were the first two signers, after Hancock, on August 2. A prolific letter writer who was regarded as an "optimistic" and "spirited patriot," Whipple wrote to a colleague on July 8, 1776: "The Declaration will no doubt give you pleasure. . . . I cannot forbear communicating the Pleasure I know You will enjoy upon Receipt of the enclosed Declaration."

As a brigadier general of the New Hampshire militia, Whipple became, in the words of one historian, a "major workhorse" in the conflict. In June 1777, he presented orders to Captain John Paul Jones, appointing him the commander of the *Ranger*, an eighteen-gun warship that took off from Portsmouth. Whipple later fought in Massachusetts, Rhode Island, and, most significantly, Saratoga, New York, the famous battle where the British, outmanned by the Continental Army led by General Horatio Gates, surrendered an army of 9,000 led by General John Burgoyne. Whipple was with Gates on October 17 when the white flag of surrender was trotted up. Later, Whipple escorted Burgoyne and many of his men to Boston to await transportation back to England. It was this victory at Saratoga that convinced France to ally themselves with the Americans.

Whipple went to war with his slave Prince, who has inspired a few legends of his own. Prince has long been identified as the man at the front of George Washington's boat in the painting *Washington Crossing the Delaware*, by Emanuel Leutze, but the claim is untrue. Although black soldiers did serve in that campaign, neither Whipple nor Prince was present during the famous Christmas crossing in 1776.

The second Prince myth concerns his freedom. As Whipple was hurrying off to war, goes the story, he told Prince to get ready.

> *Prince: Where are we going, sir?*
> *Whipple: To fight for our freedom!*
> *Prince: I have no freedom to fight for, sir.*
> *Whipple: From this moment on, you are free!*
> *Now hurry! We shall fight for our freedom together!*

And if you believe that one, there's a bridge on Ye Olde Isle of Manhattoes that you might be interested in. Historical records suggest that Prince was not freed until 1784, after the war and a year before his owner died.

Nevertheless, Prince's story highlights an oft-forgotten chapter in history. As many as five thousand black Americans are believed to have fought on the patriot side during the revolution. At first, George Washington, a slaveholder, wasn't keen on the idea of recruiting blacks. But later, as manpower shortages mounted, he agreed to enlist free blacks. At the same time, the Brits offered freedom to any slave who would fight on their side. Thousands of slaves ran away to take the British up on their offer. The Underground Railroad had nothing on the British offering freedom; more slaves escaped during the Revolutionary War than during the Civil War. Ultimately, more blacks served with the British than with the Americans. Washington and Jefferson each lost about twenty slaves who went to fight for the other side.

Toward the end of his life, Whipple became a judge. Suffering from crushing chest pains, he died in 1785 at age fifty-five, but not before requesting that an autopsy be performed to pinpoint the cause of a lifetime of fainting spells and poor health. (The postmortem revealed clogged heart arteries.) He's buried in a cemetery in Portsmouth. Prince, who died in 1797, is buried in the same cemetery—a high honor in those days. A metal marker beside the grave identifies Prince as a veteran of the Revolutionary War.

Matthew Thornton

THE SIGNER WHO LED "THE NATION OF NEW HAMPSHIRE"

BORN: About 1714

DIED: June 24, 1803

AGE AT SIGNING: About 62

PROFESSION: Physician

BURIED: Thornton's Ferry Cemetery, Merrimack, New Hampshire

New Hampshire doesn't look like much on a map, but the fifth-smallest state was actually the first of all the colonies to oust its royal governor and declare independence from Great Britain. The state's rebels made the break in January 1776. For six months before Congress declared independence, New Hampshire was arguably its own little nation. And its leader was an Irish-born physician, farmer, and eventual ferry operator named Matthew Thornton.

Thornton and his family were no strangers to persecution from outside forces. His Scotch Irish parents, having met with limited religious freedom in England and Scotland, set sail for America when Matthew was about four years old. Upon arriving, they had nowhere to go, so for the first winter they remained on the ship, parked in a chilly New England harbor. Since they were Presbyterian and not Puritan, the Thorntons rarely felt welcome in their new land. They moved from Boston to Maine and then to Worcester, Massachusetts, often finding themselves surrounded by folk who were less than keen on the Thorntons' beliefs.

Young Matthew came of age in Worcester and, like his state compatriot Josiah Bartlett, studied medicine by apprenticing with a physician there. He then settled in Londonderry, New Hampshire, established his practice, and did quite well. He bought enough land to build himself an estate. He also involved himself in political conflict from a young age; he served as a surgeon for the troops in the Louisbourg Expedition of 1745, a battle of King George's War (part of the French and Indian Wars).

Thornton first represented Londonderry in the state legislature in 1758. From there he held a variety of public posts and, again like Bartlett, was appointed a colonel in the militia and a justice of the peace by the royal governor. But once Parliament enacted the Stamp Act, his politics reached a turning point. He became a very vocal and well-known advocate of independence and also served as chairman of the local Committee of Safety, which was typically charged with protecting citizens by mounting defenses. Thornton's committee also ended up assuming supreme executive power over the colony, as we'll see.

In 1774, as the situation worsened with the Mother Country, a mob attacked a royal fort in Portsmouth, swiping its stash of gunpowder and weapons and distributing them to the local militia. By the following summer, the Royal Governor John Wentworth and his family were hiding out in the very same fort—and perhaps seeing the writing on the wall, they abandoned the colony and sailed for England. Not knowing if there would ever be a larger union, New Hampshire formed its own independent government. On January 5, 1776, Thornton's committee announced plans for a new government, and Thornton was swiftly elected the colony's president, or revolutionary executive—the first nonroyal governor, so to speak. (At this point, it was technically its own nation.)

The document created by Thornton and his committee served as New Hampshire's constitution until 1783, and it stands as the first written constitution adopted in America. While Thornton was extricating New Hampshire's government from Britain's grasp, the guys in Philly were debating, writing, and approving the Declaration of Independence. Thornton wasn't appointed to Congress until September 1776, two months after the Declaration was adopted and one month after most of the signers put their names on the proverbial dotted line. Thornton did not sign the document until November 1776.

Thornton is sometimes erroneously called the last signer of the Declaration of Independence. One myth contends that he arrived too late to sign with the others on August 2 because of bad weather, and that upon his arrival he asked for a quill so he could have the same "privilege" as everyone else—to be "hanged for his patriotism." Balderdash. First, his signature—though located in the bottom right-hand corner—was not the last. Samuel Adams took what should have been Thornton's spot below the other signers from New Hampshire, leaving Thornton to look for room elsewhere. And, to be fair, Adams took that spot because Thornton wasn't a member of Congress when the majority of the representatives signed. The honor of signing last went to Thomas McKean of Delaware, who very possibly did not sign until 1781 (see page 171). And though some argue that McKean signed as early as 1777, that still puts him after Thornton.

Though Thornton was chosen to continue with Congress in 1777, a smallpox inoculation left him with weak eyes that made it impossible for him to work. He did serve in the state legislature and as a judge for several more years before eventually retiring to run his farm and ferry and to dabble in a little writing. John Adams wrote of him: "We have from New Hampshire a Colonel Thornton, a physician by profession, a man of humor. He has a large budget of droll stories with which he entertains company perpetually." But Thornton clearly wasn't just about the laughs. In his eighties, he wrote a treatise on sin entitled *Paradise Lost; or, the Origin of the Evil called Sin, examined; or how it ever did, or ever can come to pass, that a creature should or could do any thing unfit or improper for that creature to do.* Or, is there a better title I can come up with for this document? Or, should I just stop titling it and start writing it? Or . . . oh, never mind.

Thornton lived to be eighty-nine years old. He died in Newburyport, Massachusetts, while visiting one of his daughters. On his grave is a marble slab inscribed with the summation, "An Honest Man."

II.
Massachusetts

John Adams

THE SIGNER EVERYONE LOVED TO HATE

BORN: October 30, 1735

DIED: July 4, 1826

AGE AT SIGNING: 40

PROFESSION: Lawyer

BURIED: United First Parish Church, Quincy, Massachusetts

John Adams had bad hair, flapping jowls, and a body like a potato dumpling. He was vain, cranky, and ill-tempered. He hated when people admonished him because he knew he was right—and he wasn't afraid to say so. His diaries are filled with diatribes about people who dared to question him.

Yet despite his faults, the man had several spectacular accomplishments. He loved and adored the same woman—his wife, Abigail—for fifty-four years. He lived a modest farm life and died with his accounts fully paid. He was a dedicated public servant who acted as the nation's first vice president and second president, and he raised a son, John Quincy Adams, who became president, too. And, perhaps most important, he was the single biggest force behind the American fight for independence.

The signer some called the "Atlas of Independence" was sucked into the cause by the Boston Massacre. As a lawyer living with his young family, John was asked to represent some British soldiers who had fired into an angry mob, killing five colonists. Defending such an act was an astoundingly unpopular thing to do, but John Adams was already developing a thick skin. Like his Puritan forefathers, he saw the world in absolutes, and he believed in fair trials as much as he believed in justice and freedom. Thanks to his gifted tongue, the soldiers got off, largely scot-free.

Later, as a representative of Massachusetts at the First and Second Continental Congresses, he impressed the membership with his piercing intellect and his ability to cut to the heart of any matter. Pennsylvania physician and signer Benjamin Rush said of him, "He saw the whole of a subject at a single glance, and by a happy union of the powers of reasoning and persuasion often succeeded in carrying measures which were at first sight of an unpopular nature."

Adams was not nearly so generous toward his Congressional chums. Scribbling in his diaries or dashing off letters day and night, he wrote caustic summaries of such personages as signers Benjamin Harrison ("an indolent, luxurious, heavy gentlemen, of no use in Congress or committee, but a great embarrassment to both"), Thomas Nelson Jr. ("a fat man, a speaker, and alert and lively for his weight"), and Edward Rutledge ("a perfect Bob-o-Lincoln—a swallow, a sparrow, a peacock; excessively vain, excessively weak, and excessively variable and unsteady; jejeune, inane, and puerile.") Even Ben Franklin received a backhanded compliment: "He was master of that infantine simplicity which the French call naivet[e], which never fails to charm."

Adams seemed blessed with enlightened arrogance. People who think they're always right are typically blind to their own faults. Adams was self-aware enough to know that he rubbed many people the wrong way and that this character flaw might be a political obstacle. Despite his vanity, he had the brains to step aside and let others take the credit in order to reach his ultimate goal. The best example was his manipulation of personalities to force Congress to declare independence.

He knew that the southern delegates thought he was dragging them into war, so Adams schemed to allow two Virginians to hog the official independence limelight: Richard Henry Lee, who proposed that Congress vote on the matter of independence, and Thomas Jefferson, who wrote the Declaration. In a letter written in 1822, Adams recalled the moment he passed the buck to Jefferson. In his own words:

> The subcommittee met. Jefferson proposed to me to make the draft. I said, "I will not. You should do it."
>
> "Oh! no" [said Jefferson]. "Why will you not? You ought to do it."
>
> "I will not."
>
> "Why?"
>
> "Reasons enough."
>
> "What can be your reasons?"
>
> "Reason first, you are a Virginian, and a Virginian ought to appear at the head of this business. Reason second, I am

obnoxious, suspected, and unpopular. You are very much other-
wise. Reason third, you can write ten times better than I can."

"Well," said Jefferson, "if you are decided, I will do as well as
I can."

"Very well. When you have drawn it up, we will have a
meeting."

The rest, of course, is history. Jefferson wrote the document,
and Adams signed with the others on August 2. By 1777, he had
left Congress and journeyed to France to join Franklin in persuad-
ing the French to support the Americans. A Puritan at heart,
Adams was unpopular in France's decadent court life but fared
better among the plain-speaking Dutch; he even convinced them
to lend the struggling new nation five million guilders. After the
war, Adams, Franklin, and John Jay hammered out the U.S.–Britain peace treaty, which was signed in Paris in 1783.

Upon returning from Europe, Adams received enough electoral votes to become George Washington's vice president in 1789
and again in 1792. (Until 1800, whoever placed second in presidential elections automatically became the vice president.) When
Washington graciously decided to leave office after two terms, the
nation's first bitter struggle for the presidency ensued, pitting
Adams, a Federalist, against his longtime bosom chum Jefferson,
who founded the Democratic-Republican party. Adams won and
Jefferson became second in command. Needless to say, bitterness
and rancor between the two men and their parties held sway for
the four tumultuous years of Adams's term.

There were two main incidents that marred Adams's presidency. First was the XYZ Affair, during which French agents

demanded bribes from American negotiators to stave off a war between the former allies. The affair perturbed Americans and led to further deterioration in Franco-American relations. What followed was a short, undeclared quasi-war that saw some battles in the Caribbean. Later, a misguided Adams signed into law the spectacularly unpopular Alien and Sedition Act, which was the U.S. government's first attempt to hassle immigrants and political opponents. Adams allowed himself to be convinced by members of his party that the act would allow them to muzzle the Democratic-Republicans, who were denouncing Federalists in the press. In the tension between the two parties, the friendship between Jefferson and Adams deteriorated.

When Adams lost reelection to Jefferson, it was the final straw. The two men were sworn enemies. They reconciled only when they were much older, at the urging of a mutual friend, signer Benjamin Rush. From 1812 until their deaths in 1826, they wrote each other long, philosophical letters that delighted them both. Widowed and perhaps lonely, the two Titans found solace in reminiscing about the eve of independence.

In an eerie coincidence, Adams and Jefferson died on the same day: July 4, 1826, fifty years after the adoption of the famous document. Adams, who was ninety years old, drifted in and out of a coma before dying. His last words were, "Thomas Jefferson survives." Ah, but he was wrong: Jefferson had died just hours earlier.

Samuel Adams

THE SIGNER WHOSE BREWERY WENT BUST

BORN: September 27, 1722

DIED: October 2, 1803

AGE AT SIGNING: 53

PROFESSION: Merchant, brewer

BURIED: Old Granary Burial Ground, Boston, Massachusetts

Remember that kid in school who could always be found in the middle of every fight and behind every prank? During the Revolutionary War, that kid was Samuel Adams—and his pranks included such famous stunts as the Boston Tea Party. History has anointed him the poster boy of independence (and, of course, tasty brewskies), but contemporary scholars disagree about his true role in the uprisings that led to the American Revolution.

For two hundred years, history has portrayed him as a dangerous extremist, and indeed his early Tory opponents thought him so. But his own writing bears out that he was not a bloodthirsty advocate of violent solutions to any given problem. He didn't even advocate a break from Britain until fighting broke out in 1775. But Britain's royal administrators refused to believe that Adams merely reflected the feelings of the populace; they preferred to think one man—an instigator of instigators—was stirring the pot. Remove the ringleader, they thought, and you'd have a docile public once more. They, more than anyone, helped create the legend of Samuel Adams.

From early on, Adams—once known as "Sammy the Maltster" because he was often seen traipsing through the streets of Boston carrying sacks of his family's malt on his back—rallied for the colonies' rights. He helped start a weekly newspaper, *The Public Advertiser*, in which he ranted and raved for all to read. He railed about how Parliament had overstepped its bounds with America's rights, and he supported the rights of colonists as free Englishmen. His writings and loquacious griping in the taverns made him famous among local patriots and helped popularize the cause.

When Adams's father died, Samuel inherited the family brewery, rising from "Sammy the Maltster" to "Sammy the Brewer," though the Tories still preferred to give him a good ribbing by using his old moniker. Along with the brewery, Adams received a chunk of his father's estate, but since he was about as good at holding onto money as a drunk, narcoleptic sailor, the inheritance didn't last long. The brewery went bust shortly after he took over, and Sammy was back in debt, where he remained for the rest of his life. Unable to support his family, he was forced to take advantage of his popularity as a revolutionary and rely on his wealthier friends for support. Though Adams's second wife, Dorothy Wells, managed money well, there often was little to go around. And so friends who took pity on their plight helped in little ways, like fixing up the family's home when it needed repairs.

Because of his lackluster finances, Adams was offered bribes of money, property, and fancy positions in the government that he completely despised in exchange for clamming up. Adams held on to his beliefs like a drowning man to the last life raft, which earned him even more respect from fellow patriots. He served in the Massachusetts legislature, and his voice was heard in print and at the podiums. He was dubbed a "patriarch of liberty" by Thomas Jefferson, and it's easy to see why. He had a gift for rhetoric that appealed to schooled and unschooled citizens alike. "For if our trade is taxed, why not our lands?" Adams once asked. "Why not the produce of our lands and everything we possess or make use of?" (Ironically, Adams had earlier worked as a tax collector, though his sympathies for taxpayers made him ill-suited for the post.)

Adams has long been identified as an organizer of the Sons of Liberty, an anti-British group that had a hand in many an uprising, including the Boston Tea Party. But recently, some historians have called this "fact" into doubt. On the night of the famous party, Adams was leading a protest meeting that later deteriorated. Some members of that gathering broke away, took to the streets, and stormed the ships carrying tea in Boston Harbor. Revisionist historians now say that Adams actually tried to calm the crowd and return to the meeting's business.

Even if this were true, Adams certainly refused to play nice with the king's cronies, and soon ended up on the British hit list along with his wealthy chum and benefactor, John Hancock. In April 1775, the pair was very nearly captured at a home outside

Boston where they were spending the night. Luckily they were warned, famously so, by Paul Revere on the night of his legendary ride, and they promptly went into hiding. When war broke out soon after, Adams did not fight but waged war his own way—in print and in public forums. He and Hancock were sent to Congress. Adams looked so bad in his day-to-day rags that his friends chipped in to furnish him with a suit of clothes. He cut a fine figure in Philadelphia in his new threads. A year later, he voted for independence and signed the Declaration on August 2, 1776, along with the majority of the signers.

After America earned her freedom, Adams tried (and failed) to win a seat in the House of Representatives. However, he did serve in the Massachusetts state senate. He helped draft the Articles of Confederation, the precursor to the Constitution. By 1787, when Congress embarked on improving the system of government embodied by the Articles of Confederation, Adams was in his mid-sixties, but remained a busy, busy bee. He refused to sign the new Constitution because it lacked a Bill of Rights. Without it, he felt the Constitution would give the government too much power. Finally convinced that such a bill would follow, he agreed to support the document. Late in his life, he served as lieutenant governor of Massachusetts under his old pal John Hancock. He assumed the post when Hancock died in 1793 and clung to it until 1797. He died in 1803 at age eighty-one.

If you would like to connect with the man many have called the "Father of the American Revolution," you have at least two rather interesting choices. For a back-to-nature experience, you can visit Mount Sam Adams in New Hampshire, a subsidiary peak of Mount Adams, the mountain named for Sam's cousin John. But to truly commune with Adams in his element, there is perhaps no better option than a trip to Boston. First, stop by Faneuil Hall and visit his statue, which features Adams standing defiantly, with arms crossed and chin jutted out as if to say, "Back off, mister. I just don't have your money right now." Then stop by the Old Granary Burial Ground, the nation's third-oldest cemetery and the everlasting home to Samuel Adams and several other revolutionary big Whigs, including cosigners Robert Treat Paine and John Hancock. Next to the cemetery is the Beantown Pub, where you can revel in the full-on, if somewhat morbid, Adams experience: you may chow down on a "Sam Adams" sandwich (grilled Cajun chicken, if you're curious) accompanied by a Sam Adams beer, all while looking out over his grave.

Saml Adams

Elbridge Gerry

THE SIGNER WHO GAVE US GERRYMANDERING

BORN: July 17, 1744

DIED: November 23, 1814

AGE AT SIGNING: 32

PROFESSION: Merchant

BURIED: Congressional Cemetery, Washington, D.C.

If Elbridge Gerry were working in any modern corporation, his personnel file would be stuffed with performance evaluations that all reached the same conclusion: "Does not work well with others." As vice president to James Madison, Gerry was once a heartbeat away from the highest office in the land, but today his name is best remembered in association with a word that signifies one of the worst strategies in American politics: gerrymandering.

Gerry was a well-to-do cod importer and shipping merchant by the time he accompanied his friend John Adams to the Second Continental Congress. At first glance, he looked like a lot of congressmen: slight build, smart dresser, good manners. He had a stern demeanor and slight verbal stammer. He came off a little snobbish, but people overlooked this flaw because he was, after all, a New England aristocrat. Though he voted for independence, he was unable to be in Congress on August 2 to personally sign the document. He wrote the two Adamses, instructing them to sign for him—an interesting request we've not seen among other signers—but historians agree that he signed the Declaration himself sometime in the fall of 1776.

Gerry's chief character flaw—inconsistency—came to light when the real work of waging war and nation-building began. To our jaded eyes, Gerry's behavior makes him seem like the model all future congressmen were built on, but his behavior really rankled his contemporaries. At work on military affairs, for example, he'd insist that troops receive better pay and equipment, but he inexplicably drew the line at guaranteed pensions. He detested standing armies, but he demanded that recruiters lock soldiers into long-term enlistment contracts. He said he hated military men, but he was pals with General George Washington (both were Masons). He used his insider knowledge of the military's needs to benefit his own business while denouncing war profiteers. In 1780, when Congress announced it would revise the prices it was paying war suppliers, Gerry became indignant and stormed out. He stayed away for three years, even though he was still officially a member of Congress until his term expired in 1785.

When Massachusetts sent him as a delegate to the Constitutional Convention in 1787, he angered everyone with hostile remarks and constant vacillation. First, he opposed the concepts of democracy and allowing the people to elect congressmen. Then he demanded annual elections to keep the aristocratic politicians on their toes. One attendee quipped that Gerry "objected to everything he did not propose." Gerry refused to sign the final Constitution because it lacked a Bill of Rights. Two years later, he switched sides and claimed he *did* support it, even though the Bill of Rights had not yet been added.

Fourteen years after the Revolutionary War, relations deteriorated between the United States and its former ally France over nonpayment of the former's war debt. The French seized some American ships at sea, and leaders called for war. In June 1797, seeking to avert another conflict, President John Adams sent Gerry and two other men to France to meet with the French prime minister, Charles Maurice de Talleyrand. Refusing to meet with the delegates, Talleyrand sent three agents instead. The French trio demanded bribes to arrange a meeting with Talleyrand and broker peace. Disgusted, Gerry's two colleagues returned home. Witlessly believing that his presence could avoid war, Gerry stayed in France for nearly a year. Adams finally summoned him home in May 1798, saying in effect, "Gerry, you dolt, you've been duped." By then, the damage was done. Ranking Federalists now despised their party members Adams and Gerry. Outraged that Gerry would attempt to make a deal with such oily charlatans, an anti-French mob pelted his home with rocks and shouted obscenities at his wife and children. It was all for naught. The United States entered an undeclared war with France that lasted two years.

Adams became a one-term president. Gerry defected from the Federalist camp and became a Democratic-Republican. That party nominated him for Massachusetts governor, and he was defeated four times before finally becoming the state's ninth governor. Once in office, Gerry backed a plan to creatively redraw the state senate voting districts to favor his party. A political cartoonist thought one of the districts resembled a salamander, and the process was quickly dubbed "gerrymandering." The insidious practice continues to this day and is arguably one of the biggest threats to democracy. It allows powerful parties to gain advantage by manipulating the votes in a district, shutting out minorities and other less-powerful constituencies.

The political cartoonist's influence was wide: Gerry lost reelection for governor in 1812, only to land in the White House. He had served twenty months as vice president to James Madison when he died of a severe lung hemorrhage in his carriage on the way to the U.S. Senate. The year was 1814 and Gerry was seventy-one years old and nearly broke. For years he'd neglected his finances in favor of high living and a flashy political life. He left his family so impoverished that Congress picked up the tab for a Washington burial.

Gerry was the kind of politician who inspired cynicism in the electorate, but at some point in his life he uttered a line that was idealistic, wonderful, and—dare we say?—Kennedy-esque. It's emblazoned on the tomb of this contentious signer: "It is the duty of every citizen, though he may have but one day to live, to devote that day to the good of his country."

Elbridge Gerry

John Hancock

THE SIGNER WHO SIGNED FIRST

BORN: January 12, 1737

DIED: October 8, 1793

AGE AT SIGNING: 39

PROFESSION: Merchant, shipping magnate

BURIED: Old Granary Burial Ground, Boston, Massachusetts

It's no mystery why everyone remembers John Hancock. But what's kind of sad—pathetic, really—is that someone who gave so much to the American Revolution, who took such immense risks in dedicating his life to independence, is celebrated most often during . . . National Handwriting Week.

The son of a clergyman, Hancock was born in Braintree, Massachusetts, not far from John Adams. At age seven he lost his father, and his mother, unable to keep things going on her own, sent him to live with his childless and exceedingly rich uncle, Thomas Hancock. And thus he grew up with all the privileges of a child of a shipping tycoon. He attended Boston Latin School, the oldest continuously operating public school in the country, and went on to graduate from Harvard. (Somewhere along the way, the merits of superior penmanship must have been beaten into him.) He then learned his uncle's enterprise, even traveling to England for dealings and, while there, attended the coronation of his soon-to-be enemy, George III. The import-export biz was booming. Whale oil went out, tea and silver came in. In 1764, Uncle Thomas died and Hancock inherited the business, loads of cash, and a gorgeous place on Beacon Hill. An overnight millionaire, he wasn't yet thirty years old.

For the rest of his life, Hancock was known as a remarkably generous man who spent money ostentatiously and won the adoration of Bostonians. When disasters such as fires struck, he was always the first to help the needy. He funded his alma mater, paid for street lamps and concert halls, and helped impecunious friends such as Samuel Adams feed their families. But he also had flaws. He was impossibly vain and imagined scenarios and roles for himself that he could not reasonably attain or fulfill. For example, he became peeved when Congress chose George Washington to lead the Continental Army. His frustration appears misplaced given that he had no real military experience, save the time he ran the honor guard for the Massachusetts royal governor. He and his ceremonial troops marched around in fancy uniforms that Hancock, of course, had bought for his men. Dapper and small, Hancock loved elegant clothing. In this he did not conform to one's image of a Yankee Puritan, and he later clashed famously with dour, plain, and perhaps brighter congressmen such as John Adams.

But for all his faults, he had a role to play in the drama unfolding in 1760s Boston. Like many colonists, he was outraged by the Stamp Act, though at that stage in his patriotic development he expressed his feelings in letters rather than actions. Radical Samuel Adams tried to draw him into the fray; he brought Hancock to meetings of like-minded patriots and urged him to run for office. In 1766, Hancock was elected to the Massachusetts legislature.

A few years later, one of his ships, the aptly named *Liberty*, was seized by the British, and Hancock was accused of smuggling cargo without paying the proper duty. This accusation was hardly a shock: Hancock was an unabashed smuggler at a time when smuggling was considered the only reasonable response to unreasonable taxation. Adams successfully defended him for smuggling, but the ship was seized and pressed into service as a royal vessel. A riot ensued—one that Hancock probably did not want—and the ship was burned. For better or worse, his name was thrust further into the public consciousness. Episodes such as this convinced the British to present a more forceful presence in Boston Harbor, raising tensions and eventually leading to the Boston Massacre in 1770.

In 1774, Hancock was elected president of the Massachusetts Provincial Congress and further helped the patriotic cause by raising bands of Minutemen. With so many people in need and with war looming, Hancock's popularity was rising. He was a logical choice to represent Massachusetts in the Continental Congress.

Boston Harbor had been closed by the British, and people were leaving the city in droves. In April 1775, Hancock and his pal Samuel Adams were in Lexington, staying at a parsonage that once belonged to Hancock's grandfather. Paul Revere famously rode by and scared the pants off everyone. Hancock wanted to stay and fight in Lexington—the battle that officially started the war—but Adams wisely convinced him that it would be best if they, well, ran. The two supposedly had prices on their heads, and they were being sought with particular vehemence so that they could be taken back to England, where they would likely have been tried for treason and hanged.

The two friends hid and eventually made their way to Philadelphia and Congress. In the meantime, General Thomas Gage, a military man who had taken over as governor of Massachusetts under martial law, made it clear that any colonist who came forward, renounced the patriot cause, and embraced the way of the Crown would be pardoned—except for Hancock and Adams. They were beyond forgiveness.

Folks such as Hancock—prominent, rich, influential, and dependent on shipping for their fortunes—risked much when they placed their chips on the patriots' table. This risk endeared Hancock to many, and probably made his self-involved behavior and annoying preening a little easier to tolerate. He was handily elected president of the Continental Congress and served from 1775 through 1777—throughout the resolution for independence as well as all the sniping, voting, and signing that followed. It was his task to help unify a group of quarreling, self-important men.

In the end, Hancock, as president of Congress, was the first to stick his neck out for the cause. He and the secretary of Congress, Charles Thomson, were the only men to sign the original document on July 4 before it went out to the printer, John Dunlap. One story says that Hancock announced he'd signed his name in large letters so that King George could read his signature without spectacles. This is unlikely, however, since the original document was not intended to leave the new nation. Hancock's flamboyant signature probably says more about his overall character than about any specific intent. Though John Adams resented Hancock's election to the presidency, it's unlikely that Adams could have wooed the southerners as well as did his charming and fashion-conscious friend. They probably bonded over things like tiewigs, imported silks, and the latest button designs.

After resigning as president, Hancock stayed in Congress until 1780 and focused on affairs at home. He attended the Constitutional Convention for Massachusetts and was elected its first governor, an office he held from 1780 to 1793, except for a brief two-year absence. The war had dented—but certainly not eroded—his considerable fortune. But his ill health, including perpetual and crippling episodes of gout, finally caught up with him. He died in 1793 while still in office as governor.

In a request that was out of character, Hancock had asked for a quiet funeral. He got no such thing. A huge procession, all pomp and circumstance, made its way through the streets of Boston. Bells rang, soldiers marched, stores closed, flags flew. It was a grand spectacle.

He would have loved it.

Robert Treat Paine

THE SIGNER WHO OBJECTED TO, WELL, EVERYTHING

BORN: March 11, 1731

DIED: May 12, 1814

AGE AT SIGNING: 45

PROFESSION: Lawyer

BURIED: Old Granary Burial Ground, Boston, Massachusetts

On a Monday night in March 1770, a group of British soldiers and their captain, Thomas Preston, stood watch over Boston. They were among a contingent of military men sent to the colonies to quell unrest over a variety of new taxes: taxes on paper, taxes on glass, and, most famously, taxes on tea. The colonists resented the presence of the troops and had long taunted them. On this night, however, one of the soldiers snapped, firing into the crowd of jeering Bostonians. By the time the guns were quiet, five colonists lay dead. The event became known as the Boston Massacre.

When Preston and his troops faced trial, one of their prosecutors was a young, promising attorney named Robert Treat Paine. On paper, Paine and his colleagues appeared to have an open-and-shut case: the already unpopular British soldiers had lost their composure and fired into an unarmed crowd. In fact, public opinion was so strongly weighted against the defendants that no attorney, except one, would even represent them. That lawyer? Paine's former schoolmate and future rival, John Adams.

The trial was Paine's chance to shine in a profession he had come to relatively late in life. He had spent much of his life as a young adult floundering from profession to profession. After graduating from Harvard at age eighteen, he taught school for a while. Later, he followed his family's suggestions and threw himself into the study of theology. He served as a chaplain during the French and Indian War, but he soon determined that the ministry wasn't for him, either. After the war, the confused, young Paine did what many confused, young people do today—he traveled. He went to the Carolinas, England, Spain, the Azores, and even sailed past Greenland on a whaling vessel. When he returned to Boston, he was finally ready to discover his life's calling: law. Even still, Paine was out of step with the mainstream; shockingly, perhaps, for a former divinity student, he got his girlfriend, poor Sally Cobb, pregnant and married her to make things right. They went on to have eight children together.

As a prosecutor in the Boston Massacre trial, Paine had an opportunity to make his mark, but he blew it. He was no match for Adams's quick tongue and penetrating logic. The defense lawyer argued that the crowd had provoked the soldiers, who had a legal duty to respond. The outcome was certainly regrettable, but the men had done their jobs. In the end, Preston and six of his eight men were acquitted. Two were convicted of manslaughter; they were not hanged but rather branded, somewhat absurdly, on their thumbs.

Bostonians despised the trial's outcome and added it to their ever-growing list of grievances against the Crown. Though he lost the trial, Paine was regarded as a hero among patriots for his work. He parlayed his patriotic street cred into a seat on the Massachusetts legislature, and he later served as a delegate in the First and Second Continental Congresses. His fellow congressmen found him amiable and jocular in debates, though he seldom proposed original or new ideas. If anything, he was most often heard opposing someone else's idea—a habit that won him the nickname "The Objection Maker." (Apparently "Major Paine" was already taken.) People wondered if maybe the attorney didn't have an intellectual blind spot. "He had a certain obliquity of understanding which prevented his seeing public objects in the same light in which they were seen by other people," Benjamin Rush wrote of him.

In the lead-up to the revolution, Paine maintained a desire for a reconciliation with Britain longer than many of his fellow Massachusetts delegates. Though he was a buddy of John Hancock—who was much hated by the Crown—Paine was always more moderate than either Hancock or Samuel Adams. The Adamses despised Paine's indecision on the issue of independence, and in turn Paine resented their disrespectful attitude toward him.

Paine remained influential in Congress and Massachusetts state affairs throughout his life. He was the state's first attorney general; he helped write the state's new constitution; and he later accepted Hancock's invitation to sit on the state's supreme court, where he served until his hearing deteriorated so badly that he could no longer hear cases—literally.

One of his sons—who later changed his name to Robert Treat Paine Jr.—desperately longed to become a poet. His fortunes rose and fell throughout his life, and he alienated his father by marrying an actress. (Actors were shunned by all respectable people at the time.) Junior drank, gambled, and ran up debts, though his poems earned him excellent recitation fees. Ill, indebted, impoverished, and following the script from the Bohemian playbook, the thirty-seven-year-old attorney-poet died in his parents' attic in 1811. His wounded father, the esteemed jurist, died just a few years later, at age eighty-three. He is buried in the Old Granary Burial Ground in Boston, along with his childhood friends, classmates, and fellow signers John Hancock and Samuel Adams.

Robert Treat Paine could trace his lineage back to a multitude of Paines on his father's side and Treats on his mother's side, among them a colonial governor, an acting president of Harvard, and a signer of the Mayflower Compact. Considering how scandalized he was by his son's betrothal, imagine how he would react if he knew that one of his descendants and namesakes is, in fact, an actor: Treat Williams.

III.
Rhode Island

William Ellery

THE SIGNER WHO IS TWO DEGREES FROM KEVIN BACON

BORN: December 22, 1727

DIED: February 15, 1820

AGE AT SIGNING: 48

PROFESSION: Lawyer, merchant

BURIED: Common Burial Ground, Newport, Rhode Island

With his wire-rimmed glasses and round, chunky face, signer William Ellery of Rhode Island didn't really fit the stereotype of a firebrand for liberty. He was more like a slow, steady, loyal clerk of liberty.

Though he was the son of a rich merchant and a Harvard graduate, Ellery struggled to support himself for much of his life. Love—and his fiery loins—was partly to blame. He married young, and during his long life, two wives bore him sixteen children, the second-largest brood of any signer. (Carter Braxton of Virginia tops him, boasting an impressive eighteen kids.) Not all of his progeny lived to adulthood, but suffice it to say that he had his hands full.

Early on, Ellery was forced to take on a series of jobs—merchant, customs collector, clerk of the general assembly, clerk of the court of common pleas—until, at age forty, he was finally able to study law, his dream. The job suited him and he finally prospered, with his practice stretching beyond the confines of his small colony into nearby Massachusetts. He became involved in local politics and was eventually chosen by his fellow delegates to attend the Second Continental Congress. But this unassuming gent was neither the colony's first nor its second choice to attend Congress. He was more like the accidental third runner-up. Rhode Island was represented in Congress by two men, Stephen Hopkins and Samuel Ward, the colony's former governor. Three months before he was to vote on independence, Ward contracted smallpox in Philadelphia and keeled over dead. Ellery was in.

Ultimately, Ellery, a self-described "dabbler," did not gain much fame or popularity outside his state. But he lives on in history as the man who sat and watched. He famously chose to bear witness as his fellow signers put quill to the Declaration of Independence, presumably on August 2, 1776. "I was determined," he later reported, "to see how they all looked as they signed what might be their death warrant. I placed myself beside the secretary Charles Thomson and eyed each closely as he affixed his name to the document. Undaunted resolution was displayed in every countenance."

If slow and steady wins the race, then Ellery was the tortoise among the signers, in more ways than one. He joined Congress in May 1776 and remained there for eight of the next ten years. He was a competent, well-liked individual whose skill kept him in office through various administrations. He diligently worked on several Congressional committees that would have bored other men to tears, including the committees on mail routes, war wounded, army purchases, and public accounts.

Shuttling back and forth between Philadelphia and Rhode Island could not have been easy in those days. An early writer dubbed him the "Congressman on horseback" because he often traveled at the reins of a single steed and not by carriage, as many men of means did. In those days, being a successful lawyer did not always mean one was flush with cash. Attending Congress took a toll on many men's finances, for they were forced to support themselves in Philadelphia and maintain their families from a distance, all while neglecting their businesses back home. On one trip up the coast, Ellery stayed at an inn with John and Samuel Adams, and all three Yankees noshed together on a frugal snack of bread and butter. "Had I announced myself a member of Congress," Ellery once wrote, "who would have believed me? . . . Setting aside my spectacles, there is, I am sure, no dignity in my person or appearance."

Mousy as he was, Ellery had still taken part in a momentous event—and ended up paying a price for it during the war. In 1778, British troops looted and partially burned his home during their three-year occupation of Newport. (There's no evidence that the British knew he was a signer.) Ellery and his family fled to Dighton, Massachusetts, east of Providence, where they restarted their lives. In 1786, after his long stint in Congress, Ellery hurried home to Rhode Island to shore up his income, working a series of jobs until George Washington graciously appointed him customs collector for Newport in 1790. This post provided him with financial stability and lasted until his death thirty years later. In a letter to his grandson, Ellery enumerated all the jobs he'd held over the years: "I have been a clerk of the court, a quack lawyer, a member of Congress, one of the lords of the admiralty, a judge, a loan officer, and finally a collector of the customs, and thus, not without many difficulties, but as honestly, thank God, as most men, I have got through the journey of a varied and sometimes anxious life."

Despite a fiscally stressful life, Ellery survived both of his wives and was one of only three signers to live into their nineties. In sheer longevity, he's sandwiched between John Adams, who died at age ninety, and Charles Carroll of Maryland, who died at ninety-five. But his sixteen children helped guarantee that Ellery will live forever. His descendants include William Ellery Channing, the Transcendentalist poet who hobnobbed with Ralph Waldo Emerson and Henry David Thoreau, and the author-abolitionist-attorney Richard Henry Dana Jr. In 1822, Ellery's granddaughter Elizabeth Dana Ellery married the son of Theodore Sedgwick, the fifth Speaker of the House of Representatives. Through that marriage, the Ellerys were linked to the Sedgwick clan, so that Edie Sedgwick, the late socialite-actor who starred in many of Andy Warhol's films in the 1960s, and her first cousin, actor Kyra Sedgwick, are also among Ellery's descendants. And since Kyra Sedgwick is married to actor Kevin Bacon, this makes Ellery (and the rest of the signers) a link in the popular parlor game "Six Degrees of Kevin Bacon."

William Ellery

Stephen Hopkins

THE SIGNER WITH THE WORST PENMANSHIP

BORN: March 7, 1707

DIED: July 13, 1785

AGE AT SIGNING: 69

PROFESSION: Farmer, merchant

BURIED: North Burial Ground, Providence, Rhode Island

Stephen Hopkins was as old and venerable a patriot as ever graced the halls of the Continental Congress. Though his signature on the Declaration is remarkably shaky, the man himself never wavered in his patriotic pursuits. A farmer and merchant who held almost every position of significance in his colony, Hopkins also played a pivotal role in outlawing the slave trade in his state—despite his and his brother's involvement in the execrable business.

Hopkins served the colonies early and often. He juggled public service with work with his brother Esek in the shipping business. Smaller stints on town councils eventually led him to the Rhode

Island legislature, the beginning of a long lifetime of public service. In 1754, he was a delegate to the Albany Congress. Representatives from seven colonies met in New York to discuss improving their relations with the tribes and what to do with those pesky French. The Indians sided with the French, and the final chapter in the French and Indian Wars began that same year. But all was not lost. Hopkins got cozy with one Benjamin Franklin, who was already talking up plans for uniting the colonies. Hopkins, too, was onboard with unification back then, though he and Franklin would wait a long time to see it come to pass.

In the years leading up to and following the signing of the Declaration of Independence, Hopkins served as chief justice of the superior court, established the first public library in Providence, and helped found the *Providence Gazette and County Journal* to combat the existing Tory press. In 1764 he published an article entitled "The Rights of the Colonies Examined," which was not only reprinted throughout the colonies but made its way across the pond as well, where it garnered a great deal of attention. And he served as governor ten times between 1755 and 1768.

While chief justice, he found himself ensconced in a bit of controversy. In 1772, some naughty Rhode Islanders burned the British revenue schooner *Gaspee* (read: a very big tax-collecting ship). England instructed Rhode Island to arrest the men and send them back to the motherland for trial, but Hopkins refused. After that defiant episode, there was no doubt where Hopkins stood in the developing conflict between the colonies and England.

In 1774, Hopkins became a delegate to the Continental Congress. That same year, he introduced a bill in the Rhode Island legislature to forbid the importation of slaves into the colony. It is considered to be one of the first antislavery laws in America. He fought hard for antislavery laws in Congress as well, but that battle would be left for another day. Esek, still in the shipping business, was involved in the slave trade and had the unfortunate dishonor of being at the helm for the horrendous voyage of the *Sally*, during which a huge number of slaves died. (In a slightly nepotistic move, when Hopkins later helped establish the Continental navy, he made his brother Esek commander in chief.)

Hopkins is often lauded for manumitting most of his own slaves during his lifetime, as opposed to merely granting their freedom upon his death. However, there is evidence that Hopkins's name was stricken from the roll of Friends of the Smithfield Monthly Meeting for refusing to free one of his slaves. Quakers never smiled on slavery, and Hopkins's tireless efforts to pass antislavery legislation did not make up for this transgression. Of course, the Quakers were against war, too, so he was probably bound to get the boot, no matter what.

Some find it odd and hard to comprehend that a slaveholder would introduce antislavery legislation, but this seeming paradox was rife among the signers (and others) of the day. Thomas Jefferson was perhaps the most notorious of the I-know-this-is-wrong-but-I-have-them-anyway set. Then there's Charles Carroll, Benjamin Franklin, Edward Rutledge, and the list goes on. They may have eventually come to feel that the practice was wrong, but there were greater consequences in putting their money where their legislative mouths were.

Hopkins was the second-oldest signer, after "Grandpa" Franklin, and his age shows in his signature, which is pretty wobbly. Suffering from a condition later assumed to be a form of palsy, he often had difficulty writing due to incessant shaking. While taking his turn to sign the document on August 2, the staunch patriot worked to steady his hand and uttered one of the better-known quotations from that famous day: "My hand trembles, but my heart does not!"

Hopkins entertained his fellow delegates with his wit and is sometimes referred to by the nickname "Old Grape and Guts," reportedly due to his love of drink. This delicious moniker was popularized by the Broadway musical *1776*, but its historical accuracy has been debated. Hopkins's fondness for alcohol—especially Jamaican rum—is documented elsewhere, but his habits were quite common in a time when clean drinking water was scarce, and booze was often the only available substitute. John Adams wrote that Hopkins's humor "kept us all alive" and that "Hopkins never drank to excess, but all he drank was immediately not only converted into wit, sense, knowledge, and good humor, but inspired us with similar qualities."

IV.
Connecticut

Samuel Huntington

THE SIGNER WHO BECAME THE FIRST U.S. PRESIDENT— SORT OF

BORN: July 1731

DIED: January 5, 1796

AGE AT SIGNING: 45

PROFESSION: Lawyer

BURIED: Colonial Cemetery (aka Old Norwichtown Cemetery), Norwich, Connecticut

The pantheon of U.S. presidents contains many men with unusual professions. There's a tailor (Andrew Johnson), a haberdasher (Harry S Truman), a rancher (Teddy Roosevelt), a sheriff (Chester A. Arthur), and even a peanut farmer (Jimmy Carter). But to date none of the chief executives ever worked as a cooper, or barrelmaker. However, that would change tomorrow if the Historical Society in Norwich, Connecticut, has its way and Samuel Huntington is recognized as the first president of the United States.

Huntington, one of four signers from Connecticut, was a self-made man who rose from humble origins to attain one of the highest offices during the revolutionary era. As the oldest of ten children, Huntington was expected to work the family farm and thus never went to school or college. When he was about sixteen, he apprenticed with a barrelmaker, which, considering the amount of hooch that was imbibed in those days, was a quite necessary if not glamorous profession. He was an industrious teen, borrowing books to read during his downtime, and by his mid-twenties he'd made the leap to become a practicing attorney in Norwich. A few years later he married a minister's daughter graced with the serendipitous name of Martha Devotion.

Huntington was a true Yankee: reserved, religious, formal, and dignified. A shy man, he wasn't much of a speaker, and he didn't write much or well. And yet he was a member of the Connecticut legislature when he was just in his early thirties and a judge by his early forties. Connecticut then sent him to Philadelphia as part of the Continental Congress, and he voted for independence and later signed the Declaration.

In 1779, when President of Congress John Jay was appointed as U.S. minister to Spain, Huntington was elected to replace him. He held the honored position for about two years, until July 1781, when he fell ill and was forced to return home to Martha, who devotedly nursed him back to health. Despite seesawing vigor for the remainder of his life, Huntington continued to rack up an impressive number of titles: chief justice of Connecticut's supreme court, lieutenant governor of Connecticut, and finally third governor of Connecticut. Huntington died while serving as governor, at the age of sixty-four. He was buried in the Old Norwichtown Cemetery, just fifteen miles south of where he was born.

And there he would have rested forever, another forgotten signer, were it not for the curious thing that happened while Huntington served in Congress. On March 1, 1781, the Articles of Confederation—the nation's first attempt at a constitution—went into effect, officially transforming the thirteen sovereign states into a single entity known as the United States of America. On that day, say some historians, Huntington became the nation's first "real" president when his title changed from "President of the Continental Congress" to "President of the United States in Congress Assembled." When he resigned four months later, nine other men served in that role, among them signers Thomas McKean of Delaware, Richard Henry Lee of Virginia, and that old stalwart John Hancock. Seeking to thrust its native son into the limelight—and drum up a few tourist dollars—the modern-day Norwich Historical Society has lobbied Congress to have Huntington and the nine other "forgotten presidents" formally recognized as true presidents of the United States. (Incidentally, that would make George Washington the eleventh president.)

The claim is not entirely illogical. Under the Articles of Confederation, presidents did perform a number of important tasks, such as meeting with foreign dignitaries, presiding over war councils, and signing loans. But most historians insist that the executive branch as we know it did not exist until the U.S. Constitution was ratified in 1787. Until then, the President of the United States in Congress Assembled served as a kind of presiding administrative officer. In fact, they add, the Constitution was needed specifically because the Articles of Confederation were weak. The Articles were drawn up while Americans were still in the middle of a bloody war to rid themselves of an overbearing central government, and they were deeply suspicious of once again consolidating power in the Confederation. It took the creation of the three-branch system of government, with its masterful series of checks and balances, to convince all thirteen states to give nation-building a chance.

But these protests fall on deaf ears in Huntington's neck of the woods. The citizens of Norwich and its environs have spruced up Huntington's remains to meet twenty-first-century standards. In 2003, using $31,000 in donations from local residents, the town exhumed the bodies of Huntington and his devoted Martha, refurbished their dilapidated tomb, and lovingly re-interred them in spanking-new caskets. Today you'll find them there, resting in peace for all eternity: Martha Devotion, the first First Lady, and Samuel Huntington, president, governor, signer, lawyer, barrelmaker.

Sam^el Huntington

Roger Sherman

THE SIGNER WHO SIGNED EVERYTHING

BORN: April 30, 1721

DIED: July 23, 1793

AGE AT SIGNING: 55

PROFESSION: Cobbler, lawyer

BURIED: First at New Haven Green, then moved to Grove Street Cemetery, New Haven, Connecticut

History has been quick to assign labels to those who put their name to the Declaration of Independence: the only minister, the oldest signer, the only two bachelors, and so on. But throughout the years one unique attribute has been sorely overlooked: the only cobbler.

Of course, to single out Roger Sherman solely (no pun intended) for his ability to fashion a smart, low-heeled buckle shoe is doing him an injustice. Like his fellow signers Benjamin Franklin and George Taylor, Sherman ascended from a humble background to sign not one but four important founding documents.

He spent his formative years in Stoughton, Massachusetts, where his father farmed and made shoes. Sherman had little opportunity for a formal education until he reached the age of thirteen, when a small schoolhouse opened in the area. He didn't allow his circumstances to hold him back, however; he consumed books, and a local Harvard-educated reverend, Samuel Danbar, contributed to the boy's studies. Sherman was trained in cobbling, and one popular story about his youth is that he kept a book propped open on his cobbler's bench so he could read while he worked. True or not, it makes for a swell tale.

When Sherman's father died around 1741, the family moved to New Milford, Connecticut, where one of Sherman's brothers was already living. Another swell tale—one that may very well be true—is that Sherman walked the whole way from Stoughton to New Milford, a distance of more than 150 miles, carrying his cobbling tools on his back. Once in their new hometown, the family settled in and Sherman got to work. By 1745 his aptitude for math had landed him a job as county surveyor.

He liked writing and contributed to journals, and for years he published an almanac. He and his brother soon opened New Milford's first store, and he was on his way to a new life. He found his entrée into the legal arena by chance: To help a troubled neighbor, Sherman approached a lawyer for advice on his neighbor's behalf. He presented the lawyer with notes he'd taken on the plea, and when the lawyer saw the quality of his work, he suggested that Sherman consider law as a profession. Sherman needed little convincing; he hit the books he loved so much and was admitted to the bar in 1754.

So, by his early thirties the poor son of a cobbler had entered into business for himself, married his sweetheart (Elizabeth Hartwell, from Stoughton), bought land, and started publishing his writings. To complete his accomplishments, he entered public service. He held positions as a justice of the peace and county judge, and in 1755 he joined the Connecticut colonial legislature.

In 1760, Elizabeth died, leaving Sherman to care for seven children. A year later he moved his family to Chapel Street in New Haven, across from Yale, and opened a bookstore, which allowed him to socialize with like-minded bookworms, professors, and students. Business grew. He soon married again, to Rebecca Prescott, and had eight more children, which brought his total brood to a whopping fifteen. Meanwhile, he continued to hold a variety of positions in the legislature and as a judge and also found time to serve as treasurer of Yale. The institution even granted him an honorary degree.

Sherman was a natural choice for Connecticut to send to Philadelphia as a Congressional delegate. Though moderate and essentially nonviolent, he was nevertheless a patriot. He attended the First and Second Continental Congresses from 1774 to 1781 and returned to Congress from 1783 to 1784, focusing primarily on finance. He warned about printing too much paper money and advocated higher taxes as an alternate approach.

As John Adams said, Sherman was a "good old Puritan," and he had the requisite plainness that went along with it. His presence and style as a speaker weren't flashy, but everyone listened to what he had to say. Thomas Jefferson later said that Sherman "never said a foolish thing in his life." He voted. He signed. He conquered. And still he wasn't finished.

Throughout his tenure in Congress, Sherman remained active at the state level, serving as a judge and on the committee of safety. He was elected mayor of New Haven in 1784 and held the office until 1786. Then he was drawn back into Congress for the all-important convention to sort out the Constitution, where he gave more than one hundred speeches.

Sherman played an important role in the drafting of America's three most important documents. He was on the Committee of Five that drafted the Declaration of Independence, along with Jefferson, Ben Franklin, John Adams, and Robert R. Livingston. He also helped develop the Articles of Confederation. In fact, he is the only person to have signed the Articles of Association, the Declaration of Independence, the Articles of Confederation, and the Constitution. To this last, he contributed what is called the "Great Compromise." When the smaller states were worried that a population-determined form of representation would leave them with little voice, he suggested a dual legislative system: the lower house, the House of Representatives, would be determined by proportion of population, and the upper house, the Senate, would consist of two seats for each state. Sherman's suggestion is still in use today.

By the time the Constitution was signed, Sherman was in his mid-sixties and had been active in public life for more than thirty years. Some people would be ready to retire at this point, but Sherman's Puritan work ethic wouldn't let him quit. He continued serving Connecticut at the federal level, first in the House of Representatives, from 1789 to 1791, and then as a senator, an office he held when he died in 1793. Few men could, ahem, fill his shoes.

Roger Sherman

William Williams

THE SIGNER WHO WAS CERTAIN HE WOULD HANG

BORN: March or April 1731

DIED: August 2, 1811

AGE AT SIGNING: 45

PROFESSION: Merchant

BURIED: Old Trumbull Cemetery, Lebanon, Connecticut

William Williams gave his time and his money to the independence movement. In fact, he gave his time to almost everything and everyone. He was elected or appointed to a ridiculous number of offices throughout his lifetime and held them for decades—all at the same time. He was truly a multitasker's multitasker, that William Williams.

Born in Lebanon, Connecticut, Williams hailed from a family that could afford to send him to excellent schools, up to and including Harvard University. The son of a minister, he originally studied theology under his father's tutelage. He later joined the military and served in the French and Indian War, during which time he apparently developed a distaste for the British.

He then decided to try business, specifically the mercantile trade. He opened a successful shop in Lebanon, which he ran for many years. It was perfect for him: He was constantly in the public eye and guaranteed to meet many of the region's leading citizens. Those contacts helped lure him into public service while still in his early twenties, and there he stayed. A long time. He served as a selectman (or councilman) for twenty-five years, town clerk for forty-four years, and church deacon for sixty years, plus he held various posts in the lower house of the colonial legislature for about twenty-one years. And those are just the positions he earned before the age of thirty. Oh, and he was a colonel in the militia, too.

In 1771, at age forty, Williams married Mary Trumbull (daughter of the governor of Connecticut), and they had three children. Yet even with all of his family, work, business, church, and public-service responsibilities, Williams still managed to draft the state papers for his father-in-law, Governor Jonathan Trumbull, and pen articles detailing colonists' causes for publication in various journals.

In 1775, Williams coughed up some of his own dough to help the colonists raise enough money to send Connecticut troops to fight at Fort Ticonderoga. It would not be his last generosity for the sake of the American Revolution. In 1776, he resigned his colonel's commission in the militia after being selected to replace the ailing Oliver Wolcott in Congress. Williams arrived in Philadelphia too late for the storied vote on Lee's resolution, and all the incendiary debates that preceded it, but he did sign the Declaration of Independence.

From a military standpoint, of course, 1776 was a troubling year for the patriots. The British had soundly beaten the rebels on Long Island and marched across New Jersey to Philadelphia. Sometime during this period, Williams attended a meeting for the Committee of Safety, the local organization charged with defense. One night, Williams and other members of the committee started talking about the dismal state of affairs and how the Brits seemed likely to prevail.

"Well," Williams reportedly said, "if they succeed, it's pretty evident what will be my fate. I have done much to prosecute the contest, and one thing I have done which the British will never pardon—I have signed the Declaration of Independence. I shall be hung."

One of his companions, a Mr. Huntington, quipped that *he* would escape this nasty fate by virtue of never having written or signed anything against the British government.

Offended by the man's words, Williams snapped: "Then you, sir, deserve to be hanged—for not having done your duty!"

Thankfully, the tide turned late in 1776, when Washington's troops crossed the Delaware and trounced the British forces at Trenton and Princeton. Presumably Williams stopped worrying about his own execution and started calculating a way to wrap up the war. He served in Congress from 1776 through 1778 and again from 1783 to 1784. During that time he made himself useful on the Board of War and again showed his generosity for the cause. He repeatedly opened his own home in Connecticut to soldiers in need, whether they were American troops or French officers.

Six weeks before Yorktown, the British launched a massive

attack on Connecticut. Hoping to relieve pressure on British general Cornwallis, the American traitor Benedict Arnold led a contingent into Connecticut and burned the city of New London. Williams heard of the attack, saddled his horse, and rode twenty-three miles in three hours to reach the site. He arrived too late. The city was in flames and the enemy had departed. For all his haste, Williams ended up only a witness to the destruction.

Williams continued his workaholic streak even after the war was won. As if he didn't have anything else to do, he served as a judge for thirty-four years, a responsibility begun in 1775, and as a Connecticut state legislator from 1781 through 1784. In all those years, people said that he valued punctuality so much that he was never late or absent in more than ninety legislature sessions (unless he was in Congress). At war's end, he helped frame the Articles of Confederation but did not sign them. In 1788 he was on hand for the convention that led to Connecticut ratifying the Constitution. And, fearing that he hadn't done enough to serve the common good during his lifetime, in his old age he became a member of the governor's council.

Williams lived to age seventy-nine, dying in 1811. His tombstone includes the following description: "a firm, steady, and ardent friend of his country, and in the darkest times risked his life and wealth in her defense."

Oliver Wolcott

THE SIGNER WHO MELTED KING GEORGE'S HEART (AND THEN SOME)

BORN: November 20, 1726

DIED: December 1, 1797

AGE AT SIGNING: 49

PROFESSION: Soldier, lawyer

BURIED: East Cemetery, Litchfield, Connecticut

Oliver Wolcott, one of the four signers from Connecticut, is at the center of a curious, modern-day mystery that stretches back to the week the United States became a new nation.

Wolcott was born in Windsor, Connecticut, the fifteenth child of a Connecticut royal governor. He graduated from Yale and studied law, though it's unlikely he ever practiced as a conventional attorney. He was far too busy being a major general in the Connecticut militia. Wolcott fought in the French and Indian War and later in the American Revolution. He fought in the pivotal Battle of Saratoga, recruited troops for the Continental Army's

New York campaign, defended Long Island, and quelled Loyalist raids along the coastline of his native state. A skilled negotiator, he hammered out peace treaties with various Indian tribes and confederacies at least three times and arbitrated land disputes between feuding states.

Though Wolcott clearly would have voted for independence, illness kept him away from Philadelphia as the crucial vote drew near. (Signer William Williams was sent in his place but arrived in Philadelphia too late to cast his vote with Roger Sherman and Samuel Huntington.) Later that week, Wolcott was in New York City on his way home to Connecticut when he witnessed a larger-than-life demonstration in the streets. The date was July 9, 1776. General George Washington had received a copy of the Declaration of Independence, which had just been read to his troops. At the conclusion of the reading, the troops cheered wildly, then all hell broke loose. A mob of soldiers, patriots, and ne'er-do-wells stormed Bowling Green in the Wall Street area and toppled a four-thousand-pound statue of King George III astride a magnificent horse. The statue, which was made of lead coated with a fine layer of gold leaf, either shattered or was smashed by the jeering mob. The king's head, severed from its body, was supposedly paraded on a pike and eventually shipped to London as a taunt.

When Wolcott saw the fallen statue, inspiration struck. He had the pieces collected and shipped to the port of Norwalk, Connecticut, where they were then loaded onto ox carts and rolled the sixty-odd miles to the general's home in Litchfield. There, in the orchard behind his house, Wolcott put his wife, children, and some local ladies to work melting the lead and shaping it into bullets for the war effort. Wolcott's son Frederick would later attest that his father—who was tall and muscular—took an ax and chopped some of the lead pieces himself. The Wolcotts and their merry band of melters fashioned 42,088 bullets from the statue. Laura, age fifteen, made 8,378; Mary Ann, age eleven, 10,790; and Frederick, age nine, a respectable 936. Proud Papa took the bullets to Saratoga, where he and his militia helped defeat Burgoyne with hot blasts of "His Melted Majesty."

Wolcott signed the Declaration when he returned to Philadelphia in October 1776, and in 1777 he was able to sneak away from the war long enough to add his name to the Articles of Confederation. After the war, he settled into a semipeaceful life, though he did remain active in politics. In an ironic twist, when signer Samuel Huntington died in 1796, Wolcott became the governor of Connecticut, a position his father had held forty-five years earlier—but within a radically different nation. Shortly before Wolcott died in 1797, he had the pleasure of voting for John Adams as the second president of the United States.

And there the story of Wolcott would have ended were it not for that pesky statue. About twenty-five years after Wolcott's death, people started finding pieces that were apparently never melted down. A boy digging in a field near Wilton, Connecticut, six miles from where the statue was unloaded from the ship, found a huge piece of what had been the king's saddle. Another man found a piece under the floor of his aunt's milk room. Throughout the nineteenth century, pieces kept turning up near an old swamp in Wilton: parts of an arm, a thigh, saddle straps. In the early twentieth century, people in and around Wilton were presenting pieces as gifts or inheriting them from deceased relatives. In the New-York Historical Society collection is a piece of the horse's tail. People have turned up bits of the statue as recently as the 1990s.

Clearly, from the moment the statue tumbled, New York and Connecticut citizens swiped a few mementos. Modern number crunchers note that such a large statue would have yielded far more than 42,000 bullets. To date, about 1,400 pounds' worth of the statue is still missing, and though Connecticut state archaeologist Nicholas F. Bellantoni swept Wilton with metal detectors in 1997, he found no additional pieces. In 2008, Bellantoni admitted that new technology might yield better results.

If you visit Bowling Green Park in New York City, you'll find the original fence that encircled the statue. The tops of the main posts once held crown-shaped ornaments, but all were sawn or wrenched off in that raucous celebration more than 230 years ago.

Oliver Wolcott

v.
New York

Philip Livingston

THE PRINCE OF NEW YORK

BORN: January 15, 1716

DIED: June 12, 1778

AGE AT SIGNING: 60

PROFESSION: Merchant

BURIED: Prospect Hill Cemetery, York, Pennsylvania

Had he been born in a different era, Philip Livingston would have been the Prince of New York. His family owned about 160,000 acres on the eastern side of the Hudson River, in what is now New York's Columbia County. That shakes out to about 250 square miles, or 6½ Disney Worlds. As the fifth son of Philip Livingston, he became the second Lord of Livingston Manor. In those days, "manors" were political entities, and the sheer size of the Livingston estate meant that the family automatically earned one seat in the New York royal legislature and could act as judges within their territory. It was good to be a Livingston.

Livingston, who was sixty when he signed the Declaration, had lived a long posh life by the time his opinionated personality collided with the other signers in Philadelphia. He'd graduated from Yale, married Christina Ten Broeck, a daughter of the mayor of Albany, and fathered nine children. Besides the upstate manor, he possessed two homes in New York City: one on Duke Street in Manhattan (near Wall Street) and another quaint forty-acre estate in Brooklyn Heights, where he could watch his ships carry precious British cargo in and out of New York Harbor.

He took the Livingston seat in the royal assembly in New York in 1758. Throughout the Stamp Act crisis, he maintained a moderate stance toward the British—as an importer, he was strongly tied by business to Europe and had even acted as a trader-privateer during the French and Indian War. Besides, violence and revolt gave him the heebie-jeebies. He wished those New England troublemakers would just behave and seek redress the old-fashioned way: as gentlemen. In a windy speech before the lieutenant governor, Livingston asked for what he and his fellow elite felt they deserved: to be counted as Englishmen first and taxpayers second. "We hope your honor will join with us in an endeavor to secure that great badge of English liberty," he said, "of being taxed only with our own consent; which we conceive all his majesty's subjects at home and abroad equally entitled to."

In 1774, Livingston went to Congress and immediately started to annoy John Adams. Livingston described the fight for independence as "the most vain, empty, shallow and ridiculous project." He threw up an unapproachable facade and would ignore or stonewall discussion on more leftist agendas. In August 1774, an exasperated Adams wrote of him: "There is no holding any

Conversation with him. He blusters away. Says if England should turn us adrift we should instantly go to civil Wars among ourselves to determine which Colony should govern all the rest."

Despite these views—or perhaps because of them—Livingston made certain that he served on at least four major committees in Congress, plus a board that inspected troops under General George Washington. In time Livingston's hard-line stance mellowed. By mid-June 1776, everyone in the colonies knew that the big vote on independence was approaching in the first week of July. Because British troops were bearing down on New York, Livingston delayed his departure from New York City until June 30, so he most likely missed the debate and vote for independence. Of course, it doesn't matter that he was absent on July 2, since New York abstained and did not assent until later that month. On August 2, the converted Livingston joined in signing with the other New York delegates.

Disaster dogged him just weeks later. After the Continental defeat at the Battle of Long Island—the colonies' first major battle as a new nation—on August 27, 1776, George Washington retreated to Brooklyn, where he and his officers held a brief war conference at Livingston's house. The British were moving toward New York; everyone decided to evacuate. Livingston's family fled north along the Hudson River to the small city of Kingston, where New York had moved its state capital. The British seized Livingston's homes, using one as a hospital and the other as barracks. The "hospital," Livingston's country house in Brooklyn, was later burned. Livingston, who had suffered financially during an earlier boycott of British goods, sold some property to preserve his credit.

Pity them not: the family ultimately thrived, building forty mansions along the Hudson and acquiring land whose combined area was greater than all of Rhode Island.

Livingston, however, died without knowing if the vain, empty, shallow, and ridiculous exercise in liberty ultimately paid off. In May 1778, he felt duty-bound to attend Congress despite feeling under the weather. Because British troops occupied Philadelphia, Congress was then meeting in York, Pennsylvania; with his son as his only companion, he joined the others in hiding there. He never saw his beloved Livingston Manor again. He died of "dropsy," or congestive heart failure, soon after arriving in York. Livingston was the third signer to die, after John Morton and Button Gwinnett. He was sixty-two.

William Floyd

THE SIGNER WHOSE HOME WAS TURNED INTO A STABLE

BORN: December 17, 1734

DIED: August 4, 1821

AGE AT SIGNING: 41

PROFESSION: Planter, land speculator

BURIED: Westernville Cemetery, Westernville, New York

William Floyd was Mr. Peripheral. A minor figure in the Revolution, he lived in a manner remarkably typical of many members of the landed gentry. But at the end, his life took an unexpected twist. Touched by tragedy during the Revolutionary War, he ending up seeking solace on the frontier.

Floyd was born to a rich, civic-minded family on the Long Island shore, close to Mastic Beach and across from modern-day Fire Island. The Floyds had been in America since the 1650s, and therefore one would expect the son to have received an excellent education, either grounded in the classics or possibly the law. But that was not to be.

As the eldest son in a family of nine, Floyd was expected to take over the family estate after the death of his parents. And since both his parents died while he was still in his teens, Floyd stepped into his inherited role early in life, leaving him no time for schooling. In his twenties, he married Hannah Jones, and with the help of their slaves the couple ran the family farm, caring for Floyd's siblings as well as their own children.

New Yorkers such as Floyd were slow to react to events occurring in the colonies. Indeed, New York and Georgia were the last two colonies to assume governance into their own hands. Revolutionary fervor, when it did take hold in those colonies, operated on a county-to-county basis. Floyd and men like him were conservatives, or even moderates, wary of breaking with Britain but desirous of being left alone to do as they pleased.

From his glorious estate overlooking the Atlantic Ocean, Floyd played the part of a generous host and a simple country squire who enjoyed hunting parties and long rides on horseback. Over the years, Floyd may have occasionally traveled into Manhattan for a taste of the sophisticated life. He could not help but notice that things were changing, and so he changed, albeit slowly, along with them.

Following in the footsteps of his great-grandfather, Floyd became involved in the local militia in 1760 and was active in local politics during the turbulent decade when colonists were becoming increasingly disgruntled with their relationship with Britain. By 1774, at age forty, Floyd was chosen to sit in the First Continental Congress and signed the Articles of Association, one of the first documents the colonies created to explain how they would enact boycotts against British goods.

After Floyd's initial stint in Congress, it seemed he might vanish into the woodwork. But upon returning home to Long Island, he led a militia group in a successful defense of their lands against the British at Gardiner's Bay. Thereafter, Major General Floyd was regarded as a local hero and sent to the Second Continental Congress.

Though warm, friendly, and candid at home, Floyd was shy about making friends in Congress. Perhaps he was self-conscious about his lack of education. He wasn't an abstract thinker, and he based many of his decisions on life experience. In the presence of more cultivated minds, he may have felt reluctant to speak up. Nevertheless, he volunteered for several committees, worked hard, and was admired by many fellow delegates.

On July 2, 1776, Floyd and the other New York delegates abstained from voting, pending instructions from their home delegation. The colony finally assented and accepted the Declaration of Independence on July 9, and Floyd—who is believed to have been the first New Yorker to sign—put quill to parchment on August 2, 1776. His name appears at the top of the colony's four delegates.

The Floyds, whose property sat not far from the beach, did not escape the war unscathed. Following the Battle of Long Island, a disaster for the patriots, the British occupied the narrow strip of land. Floyd warned his wife to flee, and with the help of some local fisherman she managed get herself and her children across Long Island Sound to Connecticut. Sadly, Hannah Floyd did not survive the war; she died in the spring of 1781 and is buried in Connecticut.

After the peace treaty was signed, Floyd collected his children, who were staying with friends in Connecticut, and returned to

Long Island to find that his home had been used to board cavalry horses and his livestock and crops had been taken or destroyed. Legend says that he was financially ruined for seven years, but recent research by the National Park Service (which now operates the Floyd residence as a tourist site) suggests that these claims are greatly exaggerated. Evidence of extensive damage to the house is lacking, and it appears as though Floyd was able to renovate and move on with his life. His emotional loss—Hannah's death—was greater than his material loss, though he eventually remarried, too.

Floyd served in the first House of Representatives and was a member of the Electoral College, but as he aged those political posts were secondary to his farm and family. Late in life, he had a crazy notion to see more of the country, especially the property he'd been acquiring and developing in upstate New York. (One parcel alone was 10,000 acres.) At age sixty-nine, he deeded the Long Island home to a son and moved north to the deep frontier of Westernville, New York, in what is now Oneida County. He died there on his new farm at age eighty-six. His list of descendants includes two men whose lives couldn't be more different: President Abraham Lincoln and rock legend David Crosby.

Francis Lewis

THE SIGNER WHOSE WIFE WAS IMPRISONED

BORN: March 21, 1713

DIED: December 31, 1802

AGE AT SIGNING: 63

PROFESSION: Merchant

BURIED: Trinity Churchyard, New York, New York

The oldest of the New York signers, Francis Lewis was essentially in retirement when he jumped on the independence bandwagon. He had worked hard his entire life, both personally and professionally, to get to John Hancock's table on August 2, 1776, and it took mere months for him to lose nearly everything he'd achieved in his lifetime.

Things didn't start out so great for Lewis, either. He was orphaned as a child in Wales and raised by an aunt. He did manage to get an education, in both Scotland and England, and he eventually apprenticed as a clerk in London. The small inheritance he received upon turning twenty-one was enough for him to invest in goods he hoped to sell in the New World, and off he went to seek his fortune.

He sold his wares in both Philadelphia and New York, got a business partner, Edward Annesley, and soon made a fortune in the mercantile business. He married Annesley's sister Elizabeth, and the couple had seven children, three of whom survived past infancy. He was quite an intrepid merchant, traveling as far as Russia to take care of business, and was even twice shipwrecked off the coast of Ireland.

During the French and Indian War, Lewis worked as a supplier at the British-built Fort Oswego on the shores of Lake Ontario, just north of modern-day Syracuse, New York. He was one of the 1,700 British troops captured when the fort fell to French General Louis-Joseph de Montcalm in 1756. Lewis and some others were first handed over to Montcalm's Indian allies. Supposedly Lewis's ability to speak Welsh made it possible for him to communicate with his captors, which in turn helped him secure a better fate than that of some of his fellow captives. (This remarkable linguistic feat is debated by historians.) Still, Lewis ended up in a French prison, where he languished for seven years until the end of the conflict. And once the war was over, Lewis was given a 5,000-acre land grant for his service to the Crown. He was back in the colonies and back in business.

In 1765, Lewis attended the Stamp Act Congress before retiring to his home in Whitestone, Long Island. He remained one of the big Whigs in the New York Sons of Liberty and joined a variety of patriot groups protesting the injustices by the Crown. He was elected to Congress in 1775 and put his business sense to work on a variety of committees, including marine affairs, foreign affairs, and the Board of Admiralty. He also helped procure supplies for the struggling troops. Lewis generally didn't speak up much in Congress, but he did make a strong case in defense of George Washington during an incident known as the Conway Cabal, in which several patriot military officers and congressmen sought to replace Washington as head of the colonial forces. The cabal was quashed and most of the parties involved apologized to dear old George.

When Lewis and his peers signed the Declaration of Independence on August 2, 1776, the New Yorkers did so knowing full well that the British were preparing to pounce on the shores of their lovely colony. They weren't wrong: shortly after the signing, the British attacked Long Island. A battleship fired on Lewis's home while his wife and their servants were still inside. In one famous anecdote, after a shell struck near where Mrs. Lewis was standing, a servant yelled for her to run. The plucky, unruffled Mrs. L stood her ground, reportedly remarking, "Another shot is not likely to hit the same spot." Shortly after, troops burst through the door and started ransacking the house. One soldier snatched what looked like gold buckles off Mrs. Lewis's shoes and was disappointed to discover that they were fake. "All that glitters is not gold," she reportedly snapped.

The Lewis home was destroyed and the brave Mrs. Lewis was dragged off and cast into a New York prison. She was about sixty years old at the time, so it must not have been easy for her. She was denied a bed, a change of clothing, and decent food for weeks, until one of her slaves reportedly tracked her down and managed to slip some food, clothing, and letters to her. In retaliation, George Washington arranged for the wives of two prominent Philadelphia Tories to be placed under house arrest so that they could be swapped for Mrs. Lewis. She was finally released but not permitted to leave New York City. With her own health failing, she tended to her slave, who had fallen ill. He later died.

It's hard to calculate how many years a stay in a dank, dark colonial-era prison will take off your life, but in Mrs. Lewis's case it's likely to have been several. She died in 1779, at about age sixty-four, roughly two years after her release from prison. Her story is perhaps the most poignant of all the wives of the signers. To make matters worse for the family, of the three children who survived to adulthood, their only daughter married a British naval officer on the sly—after Lewis refused to give his consent—and took off for England. Ouch.

The grieving Lewis stayed on the Board of Admiralty until 1781 and then called it quits. He didn't bother to rebuild his Long Island home after the British destroyed it; rather, he finished off the remainder of his days living with his sons. He was almost ninety years old when he died.

Lewis Morris

THE SIGNER BURIED IN ONE OF AMERICA'S POOREST NEIGHBORHOODS

BORN: April 8, 1726

DIED: January 22, 1798

AGE AT SIGNING: 50

PROFESSION: Planter

BURIED: Morris Family Vault, Saint Ann's Episcopal Churchyard, Bronx, New York

Anyone visiting the neighborhood of Morrisania in the South Bronx will find it hard to believe that it was once the site of signer Lewis Morris's grand estate. Today's public housing projects and boarded-up buildings don't reflect how the estate looked at the height of its glory—but they do perhaps suggest what the place looked like after the British finished trashing it.

The Morris family had already established their name well before their ranks included a signer of the Declaration of Independence. Lewis Morris's grandfather was the royal governor of New

Jersey, and the future signer was also related to a chief justice of New York, a lieutenant governor of Pennsylvania, and various other men of influence. Add a land grant of a few thousand acres north of New York to their unparalleled social position and Morris's family was set for life.

After an education at Yale, Morris went home to help his father look after the family's affairs. Already loaded, he padded his reserves even further upon marrying Mary Beekman Walton (as in New York's Beekman Place, Beekman Street, Beekman Tower, etc.). Then, when Morris was thirty-two, his father died and Morris became the third Lord of Morrisania Manor (a title that sounds like it could be the name of a colonial-era soap opera).

All the New York signers were financially well-off, but Morris was the picture of aristocracy. Handsome, rich—it's no wonder he was popular. So why on earth would a man with such privilege team up with a bunch of kooky revolutionists? He was hardly suffering from the actions of the British, and most of the folks in his neighborhood were Loyalists.

Morris's conversion didn't happen overnight. His public service began in the provincial assembly. One of the better examples of his discontent with the changing relationship to the Crown came when New York was hosting a large garrison of British troops, who were there theoretically to protect the American colonies. The Crown intended to tax New Yorkers to support the troops, and when the assembly refused to vote in favor of this measure, the governor requisitioned the money anyway. Morris was not happy with this outcome, and, more important, he was not quiet about it.

In 1774, when the colonies were choosing delegates to send to the Continental Congress, Morris was not selected as a representative. New Yorkers still wanted to make peace with the Crown, and voters considered Morris too unlikely to support compromise. But by spring 1775, circumstances had changed dramatically. The Battle of Lexington had taken place, and a strong voice was needed in Philadelphia. This time, Morris was sent. Ironically, he wasn't a big talker in Congress, but he did work on the ever-important committees to secure munitions for the troops. The never-ending search for ammunition and gunpowder was Morris's primary concern.

In June 1776, Morris took a leave from his duties with Congress to command the militia in Westchester, New York, as a brigadier general. (He would be a major general by the time he retired.) He missed the big vote on Lee's famous resolution—but he really didn't miss much. New York was the only colony to abstain from voting on July 2. The delegates weren't getting enough direction from their colony and therefore were unwilling to decide one way or the other. But just a week after the vote passed, Morris helped lead New York in approving the Declaration of Independence, which it did on July 9. Only with New York's assent did the Declaration then became a "unanimous" Declaration of Independence. When he returned to Congress in September, Morris signed the document.

He probably saw what was coming next, which is what makes Morris so admirable. It wasn't that the British were targeting the fifty-six signers for their actions (though their Tory neighbors were happy to point troops in the right direction). No, the British were about to invade New York, and an estate such as Morrisania was not only a fine objective, but also a close and handy target. The house was trashed, extensive stands of trees were burned or cut down for firewood, cattle were slaughtered to feed the troops, and the tenants and slaves who could get away ran off, which was probably worse for those poor folks than it was for the Morris family. Benjamin Rush, who called Morris "a cheerful, amiable man," said that he "suffered the loss of many thousand pounds by the depredations of the British army, upon his property near New York without repining. Every attachment of his heart yielded to his love of his country."

After the war, Morris served as a judge and as a state senator and lobbied hard behind Alexander Hamilton in an effort to ratify the Constitution. He was not ruined financially by the war, and in fact he spent a lot of his time and money working to restore his estate. He was ultimately successful and ended up spending the rest of his life on the restored property. He was buried at Morrisania—the family vault located in what's called the Mott Haven neighborhood today—in the churchyard of what became St. Ann's Church of Morrisania and is known today as St. Ann's Episcopal Church. The manor house that was Morris's pride and joy is long gone. The church sits on a lovely large green expanse, one of the few in a neighborhood that is the heart of one of the poorest congressional districts in the country.

VI.
New Jersey

Abraham Clark

THE SIGNER WHOSE SONS WERE IMPRISONED

BORN: February 15, 1726

DIED: September 15, 1794

AGE AT SIGNING: 50

PROFESSION: Lawyer, surveyor

BURIED: Presbyterian Church Cemetery, Rahway, New Jersey

Abraham Clark had a modest upbringing compared to some of the other more prosperous and influential signers. But for someone who had a lot less to lose over the course of the Revolutionary War, Clark seemed to receive more than his fair share of suffering.

A Jersey boy from birth and the only child in a farming family, Clark did not receive much formal education. Yet, he made the most of his limited access to teachers and books and found work as a local surveyor and resident go-to guy for legal advice. Though apparently he was never admitted to the bar, Clark was known as the "Poor Man's Counselor" due to his willingness to help folks with land disputes, mortgages, and other small legal matters, often for no payment. He was a hero of the middle class. His generosity and solidarity with everyday folk made him exceedingly popular, and he soon occupied a variety of public offices.

By 1774, he was firmly entrenched in the patriot movement, serving on the New Jersey committee of safety and attending various revolutionary conventions. After helping to draft the New Jersey constitution, he was elected as one of the five upstart men who made up the "new" New Jersey delegation that showed up in Philadelphia in June 1776.

Clark had little patience for pomposity and posturing, to which, of course, he was probably overexposed once he got to Congress. Signer and chronic diarist Benjamin Rush once wrote that Clark was "a sensible but cynical man. He was uncommonly quick sighted in seeing the weakness and defects of public men and measures." But he was a patriot through and through, and he happily voted for independence. He signed his name on the Declaration along with the others, no matter how he felt about them. Clark knew what the signers were getting themselves into, and soon afterward wrote to his friend, Colonel Elias Drayton: "As to my title, I know not yet whether it will be honorable or dishonorable; the issue of the war must settle it. Perhaps our Congress will be exalted on a high gallows. . . . I assure you, Sir, I see, I feel, the danger we are in."

He knew the danger his family was in as well. Clark had two sons, Aaron and Thomas, captured during the war. It's believed Thomas was tossed aboard the notorious prison ship *Jersey*. Prison ships made regular prisons look like the Ritz, and the *Jersey* was one of the worst. A veritable potpourri of dysentery, smallpox, and any other kind of scurrilous contagion of death imaginable, the vessel was like a floating morgue, with scores of prisoners dying and being dumped overboard to clear the rancid decks. Clark's son Aaron was thrown in a New York dungeon called the Sugar House, and the other prisoners—themselves in dire straits—felt so bad for his condition and lack of nourishment that they reportedly passed him food through a keyhole. (You know things are going badly for you when starving inmates are poking moldy bread through your keyhole.) How his sons ultimately fared is sketchy. Some sources say Congress ordered retaliation that freed Thomas. Less is known about Aaron's fate. Other sources maintain that a third son, Andrew, may have also died aboard the *Jersey*.

Clark continued to serve in Congress on and off until the end of the war, at which point he moved to the state legislature. He attended the Annapolis Convention of 1786, at which representatives of five of the thirteen states gathered to address grievances that had arisen over the cumbersome Articles of Confederation. Representatives met again at the Federal Convention in 1787 to hammer out a new, improved system of government: the U.S. Constitution. Poor health kept Clark from attending, but he opposed the Constitution until the Bill of Rights was added.

In 1787 he returned to the Continental Congress, but he stayed in New Jersey in 1789 to focus on the state's accounts with the federal government. He capped off his public service as a representative of New Jersey under the new federal government, from 1791 to 1794. In summer 1794, Clark was watching some men build a bridge on his lands in what is now Roselle, New Jersey, when he suddenly felt ill. Intuiting that he had suffered a bout of severe sunstroke, he staggered to his carriage and got himself home. There, he was put to bed and died hours later. He was sixty-eight.

Abra Clark

John Hart

THE SIGNER WHO SLEPT IN CAVES

BORN: Fall 1713

DIED: May 11, 1779

AGE AT SIGNING: 65

PROFESSION: Farmer, mill owner

BURIED: First Baptist Church Cemetery, Hopewell, New Jersey

"Honest John" Hart was a New Jersey farmer who owned about four hundred acres and a couple of grist and saw mills. His neighbors thought highly enough of him to send him to Congress, which seemed like a really great idea—until the day Honest John woke up to find himself running for his life, trying to stay a few steps ahead of the British troops.

Hart's birthdate is unclear, though it's believed he was born in Hopewell, New Jersey. His father was a minor hero—minor to history, though much beloved and honored by his New Jersey neighbors—who on behalf of the British raised a corps of volunteer soldiers, the "Jersey Blues," to fight in the French and Indian

War. They never saw action, and Hart's father was left deeply in debt paying his men while they waited endlessly for their orders. His son inherited his father's sense of duty to country.

Though he was not educated, Honest John went out of his way to interest himself in the affairs of the world outside his farm in Hunterdon County. His plain speech and uncomplicated manner must have struck a chord with a number of New Jersey's leading citizens, who were no doubt cut from the same cloth. Long before the word *revolution* danced on people's lips, Hart served in provincial (i.e., royal) assemblies and congresses, and he had even served as a judge. (Imagine that job interview: "No education? No law school? No problem, here's your robe.") Clearly this was a time when one's reputation as a fine individual meant more than the type of schooling one received. "A plain, honest, well meaning Jersey farmer," signer Benjamin Rush wrote of Hart, "with but little education, but with good sense and virtue enough to pursue the true interests of his country."

In 1765, Hart left his home and traveled to New York to attend the secret Stamp Act Congress, in which nine of the thirteen colonies drew up grievances against the Crown. The elite of New Jersey had long sided with the king on the issue of taxation. In fact, the New Jerseyans who were sent to the First and Second Continental Congresses largely pooh-poohed all talk of a radical break with Britain. But the tide was turning against them. Popular support for separation was growing in the colony, and Hart, the simple but politically active farmer, more closely embodied the sentiments of the New Jersey populace. He opposed, for example, outside taxation and the stationing of royal troops in the colonies.

In June 1776, New Jersey's Provincial Congress canned the Tories who'd been representing the state at the Second Continental Congress and sent five pro-independence men to Philadelphia in their place. The new representatives were the Reverend John Witherspoon, Abraham Clark, Richard Stockton, Francis Hopkinson, and John Hart, who was the oldest and least educated of the bunch. They arrived in Philadelphia at the end of June, just in time for the debates. On July 2, all five cast their votes for independence, and all five signed the Declaration on August 2. Hart then returned to New Jersey, where he was elected to serve on New Jersey's first general assembly governed by a new state constitution, and where he was inexplicably elected—out of all those fancy-pants lawyers with lofty pedigrees and schooling—as the state's first speaker. This sheds remarkable light not only on Hart's character, but also on the composition of the elected body at the time.

But despite all his triumphs that summer, 1776 wasn't a great year for Hart. In October, Deborah Scudder Hart, his wife of thirty-six years and the woman who had borne him thirteen children, fell sick and died. In November, the British entered New Jersey, and by December, they were in Hart's neck of the woods. When the British drew near his home, the still-grieving widower sent his young children to stay with friends and then scampered to nearby Sourland Mountain. Legend says Hart slept in caves, dog houses, and the snowy fields for a year while the British plundered his lands and home, hunting him—as one historian says—"like a noxious beast." Modern historians do think he sought shelter for a time in a rock formation in the region, but his total days on the run would have been fewer than a month. That said, it couldn't have been fun for a man in his sixties to undergo such emotional and physical stress.

Legend also says the British destroyed Hart's home and in turn his life, but this is untrue. The house and farm were probably plundered, but they weren't harmed enough to ruin him. We know the farm was in working order shortly after the battles in New Jersey because in June 1778—one and a half years after Hart's runaway adventure—he generously hosted Washington and allowed 12,000 of Washington's troops to camp in his fields.

Hart appears to have survived his ordeal well. He continued to serve in the assembly and was reelected speaker. Though legend once again has a dramatic tale about the end of Hart's life, his death was not caused by sheer exhaustion, a broken heart, or a crushed spirit at the hands of the British. Rather, Hart died at age sixty-eight from an entirely mundane bout of "gravel," another name for kidney stones. He was buried in a Hopewell churchyard on land that he himself had probably donated to the church. Despite that the date of Honest John's death is widely known, his modern tomb-stone incorrectly reports it as 1780.

Francis Hopkinson

THE SIGNER WHO DESIGNED THE U.S. FLAG

BORN: September 21, 1737

DIED: May 9, 1791

AGE AT SIGNING: 38

PROFESSION: Lawyer, musician, Renaissance man

BURIED: Christ Church Burial Ground, Philadelphia, Pennsylvania

Benjamin Franklin and Thomas Jefferson are the classic examples of colonial-era Renaissance men who successfully dabbled in such various fields as art, science, and writing. But they were hardly the only ones. Dabbling, it seems, was what rich, well-educated men of the time did when they were bored with their chosen professions.

Francis Hopkinson, one of the five signers from New Jersey, was ostensibly a lawyer. But he was also a mathematician, chemist, physicist, mechanic, musician, and artist. He wrote what was arguably the first American opera. He built a keyboard for Benjamin Franklin, invented musical instruments, played a mean organ and harpsichord, and dedicated a book of his "airy and dainty airs" to his pal George Washington. Hopkinson also wrote the music for the earliest surviving secular American song, titled "My Days Have Been So Wondrous Free." For this and other ditties, Hopkinson would later claim for himself the mantle of "first national composer," a title subject to debate among music scholars to this day.

And this, alas, is the theme that runs through Hopkinson's life. He was a lawyer with the soul of an artist. More than anything, he appears to have craved recognition for his artistic output, but he never got what he so ardently desired. This is especially true when it comes to what was probably his greatest contribution to his nation: the American flag.

Hopkinson was born in Philadelphia, the son of Thomas Hopkinson, who was such bosom buddies with Benjamin Franklin that they founded the University of Pennsylvania together. Francis was a member of the very first class that graduated from the college. After graduation, he initially amused himself with legal positions in service to the Crown, but over time, as he became more interested in the notion of the colonies breaking with Britain, he resigned these positions. He moved to Bordentown, New Jersey, married one of the local Borden girls, and fathered five daughters. He was sent to the Second Continental Congress as a delegate for New Jersey, and he voted for independence and signed the Declaration in 1776.

In March 1780, Hopkinson took a job as Treasurer of Loans in the Treasury Department of his fledgling nation. When he wasn't writing rabble-rousing, patriotic songs or drawing caricatures of his fellow congressmen, he put his artistic talents to use designing seals for various agencies. He was on one of the committees tasked with designing the Great Seal of the United States: the stern eagle clutching an olive branch with thirteen arrows in its talons. (Three committees actually worked on this design. Hopkinson's team contributed the eagle's stars-and-stripes shield, the six-pointed stars above the eagle's head, and the olive branch.) He cranked out pencil sketches of seals for the Treasury and the Board of Admiralty (the Navy's governing body) and designs for U.S. currency, a naval flag, and even a United States flag.

No sketches of Hopkinson's flag design exist, but we do have the original description, which called for thirteen red and white alternating stripes and thirteen white stars on a field of blue. In Hopkinson's original design, the stars were six-pointed and arranged in rows.

This staggered arrangement of stars proved to be somewhat controversial. Look closely at the stars, and you'll see that they easily form crosses and diagonals. To the eyes of early Americans, this was uncomfortably similar to the design of Great Britain's flag:

So the stars on Hopkinson's flag were configured into a circle, which banished the similarity to the British flag and also suggested that no one colony or state was greater than any of the others.

Of course, this version looks remarkably similar to the one supposedly sewn by Betsy Ross. According to Betsy's story, she was presented with a design for a flag with six-pointed stars, but she convinced the gentlemen who hired her—George Washington allegedly among them—that a five-pointed star would be a wiser choice since she could cut it out of fabric with one snip. Was Hopkinson's the design sewn by Betsy Ross? We'll never know since records from that time are frustratingly murky. But some historians question aspects of Ross's story. While it's clear that she did sew flags during that period, it's not certain that she sewed the first U.S. flag. The chief evidence we have to support her story are affidavits sworn out more than a hundred years after the alleged commission. By then, Betsy wasn't around to speak for herself, so the affidavits were signed by her descendants, who were hardly impartial.

On the other hand, we do know that Hopkinson almost certainly designed some version of the flag because he famously sent Congress a bill for his services, asking for "a Quarter cask of the Public Wine" as payment for his work. All the poor guy wanted was a little free booze and a pat on the back. But Congress dissed him, saying that as an employee of the Treasury, he was expected to do such things as part of his regular pay. Insulted, Hopkinson resubmitted his bill, and the matter dragged on for another year before he resigned his office in high dudgeon. Though he was never paid, historians point out that Hopkinson is the only person in the minutes of the Continental Congress credited with having designed a U.S. flag.

Despite the injustices he suffered, Hopkinson lived through the war relatively unscathed, though his home did suffer a ransacking by Hessian soldiers in December 1776. After the war was over, Hopkinson received a package containing a book that had been stolen from his library during the incursion. Either the finder or the original plunderer scrawled a message on the bookplate, saying that the books in Hopkinson's library proved that he was a learned man who deserved to get his property back.

In his later years, Hopkinson served as a federal judge until he died of an epileptic seizure at the age of fifty-three. He was buried in Philadelphia's Christ Church Burial Ground. The gravestone took a beating over the years, and in the twentieth century there was considerable question whether he was in fact buried there. In the 1930s, the remains were exhumed and inspected by a University of Pennsylvania anatomist. The examination suggested that the remains were in fact Hopkinson's, and they were reburied under a more fitting and lasting memorial. In death he finally got the credit he longed for in life. The bronze plaque above his grave proclaims to the world that he was the "Designer of the American Flag."

Richard Stockton

THE ONLY SIGNER WHO RECANTED THE DECLARATION

BORN: October 1, 1730

DIED: February 28, 1781

AGE AT SIGNING: 45

PROFESSION: Lawyer

BURIED: Stony Brook Quaker Meeting House Cemetery, Princeton, New Jersey

From the way he wrote about public service, you'd think Richard Stockton wouldn't touch politics with a ten-foot pole. "The public is generally unthankful," he once wrote, "and I will never become a Servant of it, till I am convinced that by neglecting my own affairs I am doing more acceptable service to God and Man."

In truth, why should he put his neck out for the madding horde? Stockton, like many a prep-school grad, had a cushy life. He was married to the poet Annis Boudinot, worked in a prestigious law firm in Newark, lived in his father's mansion in Princeton, and spent his free time raising horses and collecting art. Who indeed would ruin such a life for a chance at independence?

Well, Stockton did. As a lawyer, he could not help but be impressed by some of the more persuasive arguments for the break with Britain. As a member of the reigning elite—his father was a wealthy judge and landowner who donated the lands on which Princeton University was built—he would have constantly rubbed elbows with other rich, powerful men who wanted to shuck off the royals in favor of a new nation.

Though Stockton originally favored a scenario in which Americans ruled themselves but swore allegiance to the king, he cast aside that idea the moment he and the other four Jerseymen walked into Congress in June 1776 and heard John Adams speak. All five members voted yea on July 2. It's unknown when Stockton signed the final document; it may have happened after August 2.

A cool cucumber in the courtroom, Stockton never indulged in cutthroat tactics. Signer Benjamin Rush, Stockton's son-in-law, described him as "an enlightened politician, and correct and graceful speaker. He was timid where bold measures were required. . . . He loved law, and order." But he had compassion, too. Sent with signer George Clymer of Pennsylvania to inspect troops in upstate New York in fall 1776, Stockton was appalled that New Jersey's fighting men did not have adequate supplies. "There is not a single shoe or stocking to be had in this part of the world," he wrote later to signer Abraham Clark, "or I would ride a hundred miles through the woods to purchase them with my own money."

He later tried to fulfill that promise. Hearing that the British were drawing close to Princeton, Stockton returned home to his family's estate, Morven. First, he helped feed, clothe, and supply the American soldiers in the area. He waited until they were all gone before he finally took his wife and children to stay with friends in Monmouth County, about thirty miles away. Someone there recognized him and betrayed him to the enemy. One night, while sleeping, he was rousted from bed by Loyalist militants and taken prisoner. He was jailed first in Perth Amboy, New Jersey, and then in New York City.

Hearing that Stockton was suffering and had fallen ill in prison, Congress passed a resolution instructing Washington to try to gain his release, possibly via a prisoner exchange. Many historical accounts credit Stockton's release to Washington's negotiations, but evidence from Stockton's friends suggests he was released for another reason. At the time, Britain's Admiral Lord Richard Howe and his brother, General William Howe, began offering pardons to rebels who would swear allegiance to the king and cease their war efforts. About 4,800 Americans availed themselves of this offer. In a letter dated March 1777, Stockton's friend and fellow signer John Witherspoon states that Stockton "signed Howe's declaration" and that he was back at Morven, sick from cold and exhaustion and much maligned by local gossips for his "action."

Legend also says that the grand estate Morven was destroyed during the British occupation, causing the family to fall into poverty. This is all just hysterical hyperbole. The home may have been damaged, but it was hardly destroyed. Nor did it pass out of the family's hands due to a sudden dearth of finances. Stockton family members lived at Morven well into the twentieth century, when the home became the official residence of the New Jersey state governor. It served that function until 1982, and today it is a museum located on Stockton Street in Princeton.

Stockton's month-long imprisonment did not kill him, but it

did weaken him tremendously. In fall 1779, a letter from a relative states that doctors had finally given him a clean bill of health, though it was destined to be short-lived. The previous year, a cancerous growth had sprouted on Stockton's lip. He underwent painful surgery without anesthesia to remove the tumor, but the malignancy spread to his throat and finally killed him in 1781, a few years before the war's end. He was only fifty years old.

Stockton is arguably the only signer who was persecuted because he signed the Declaration, not because of the general hazards of war. Most history books gloss over his recantation in favor of the prison exchange story, as if that ending were a more fitting tribute to the man's memory. For what it's worth, Stockton did swear his allegiance to the United States again in December 1777. Though his neighbors may have trashed his name, his friends and colleagues understood how he'd suffered in prison and that he'd only accepted his captors' terms to gain his freedom. George Washington consoled Stockton's widow, writing, "Be assured we can never forget our friend at Morven."

Today there are several notable tributes to Stockton, including a statue in the Capitol in Washington, D.C., a college bearing his name at Rutgers University, and a quaint New Jersey hamlet. In a more dubious honor, he alone—out of all five of the signers from New Jersey—is honored with a rest stop on the New Jersey Turnpike.

John Witherspoon

THE SIGNER WHO WAS ALSO A MINISTER

BORN: February 5, 1723

DIED: November 15, 1794

AGE AT SIGNING: 53

PROFESSION: Minister

BURIED: Presidents' Lot, Princeton Cemetery, Princeton, New Jersey

Despite various assertions to the contrary, and though several of the signers were former clergymen of some stripe, John Witherspoon of Scotland was the only true, active minister in Congress. But his position as head of one of America's oldest universities ensured that his influence was felt well beyond the pulpit.

Educated at the University of Edinburgh, Witherspoon began preaching in 1743, married Elizabeth Montgomery in 1748, and started raising a family. A skilled orator and a keen writer, he soon made quite a name for himself through his moving sermons and pointed texts. News of his presence and intelligence spread across the pond, where a printed version of his noted sermon, "Trial of Religious

Truth by Its Moral Influence," was apparently a colonial blockbuster.

One of those interested in Witherspoon's success was signer Richard Stockton, who was then acting as trustee of the College of New Jersey (later known as Princeton). Stockton traveled to Europe and asked Witherspoon to serve as the new president at his college. Elizabeth, who was no fan of ocean crossings and had heard tales of wild lands in the colonies, forced her husband to decline. But once she was enticed by the charms of yet another future signer, then medical student Benjamin Rush, she consented to the journey. Years later, these three men not only would sign the Declaration together, but Witherspoon would preside over the marriage between Rush and Stockton's daughter Julia.

The Witherspoon clan arrived at Princeton in 1768, and the new president immediately made an impact. He increased the endowment, revamped the curriculum, and began to turn Princeton into a force to be reckoned with. Under Witherspoon's reign, Princeton was a hotbed of developing patriots (or perhaps a mire of treasonous teachings, depending on your political leanings). The literary and debate societies, Whig Hall and Clio Hall, became the loquacious breeding grounds for future political giants James Madison and Aaron Burr, both of whom studied under Witherspoon's tenure. Scrutiny and debate over new schools of thought, including the Scottish Enlightenment, moral philosophy, and the Common Sense philosophy, helped Witherspoon make his tenure at Princeton influential and successful.

And then came politics. As a Scotsman, Witherspoon's dislike for the English got off to a healthy start long before he landed in the colonies. His sermons, writings, and local activities soon led to his election to the provincial legislature. In 1774, he published an essay titled "Thoughts on American Liberty," which left little question about where the good minister stood on the subject of independence: "The great object of the approaching Congress should be to unite the colonies, and make them as one body, in any measure of self-defence, to assure the people of Great Britain that we will not submit voluntarily, and convince them that it would be either impossible or unprofitable for them to compel us by open violence."

By 1775, he was no longer limiting his participation in the revolutionary movement to writings and sermons. He became an active member of various committees in the provincial legislature, and in early 1776 he helped establish the new constitution for New Jersey. Perhaps most important, he led the movement to remove Royal Governor William Franklin (Benjamin Franklin's estranged, illegitimate son), which led to the need for a newer, more radical New Jersey delegation in the Continental Congress. And so Witherspoon took his place among the "five independent souls," as John Adams described them, who traveled from New Jersey to Philadelphia in late June.

During the animated discussions over the fate of the colonies' self-rule, a fellow delegate happened to say that America was not yet "ripe" for independence. To this, Witherspoon summoned all the muster and influence of his pulpit-honed authoritative presence and bellowed, "In my judgment the country is not only ripe for the measure, but in danger of becoming rotten for the want of it!"

Witherspoon served in Congress until 1782. During his tenure, he was on far too many committees to list, including the board of war and the very popular (if not-so-subtly-named) committee of secret correspondence, a kind of colonial CIA that was charged with collecting foreign intelligence via letters received from friends overseas. He also participated in the debates on the Articles of Confederation. He later served in the New Jersey state legislature and, in 1787, was part of the convention that ratified the federal Constitution.

Witherspoon suffered two great losses during the war. The first, and more devastating, was the loss of his son James at the Battle of Germantown. The other was the ransacking that his college endured at the hands of the British, including the burning of books (some claim hundreds, others say thousands), many of which Witherspoon had brought with him from Europe. After the war, he worked to put Princeton back together, but he never saw it fully restored in his lifetime. (At the time of this book's publication, Princeton University appeared to be doing just fine.)

Through all of the revolutionary hubbub, Witherspoon always remained doggedly true to his calling as a man of the cloth. He was a major player in the national reorganization of the Presbyterian Church and served as moderator of the opening session of its first general assembly in 1789.

Elizabeth Witherspoon died that same year, and two years later Witherspoon raised a few eyebrows in the pews when he married a twenty-four-year-old widow named Ann Dill. He was then about sixty-eight, but clearly not lacking spunk; they had two children, though only one survived past infancy. Witherspoon died in 1794 and was buried in the Presidents' Lot at Princeton Cemetery.

VII.
Pennsylvania

John Morton

THE FIRST SIGNER TO DIE

BORN: About 1724

DIED: About April 15, 1777

AGE AT SIGNING: About 52

PROFESSION: Farmer, surveyor

BURIED: Old St. Paul's Cemetery, Chester, Pennsylvania

John Morton walked onto history's stage for a brief, shining moment, did something momentous, then exited without so much as a farewell bow. On July 2, 1776, Morton was the man who threw Pennsylvania into the "yea" column, shifting the results of the vote on the resolution unanimously in favor of independence.

Morton's family was of Finnish and Swedish origin; he was born on a Pennsylvania farm shortly after his father's death. Luckily for him, his mother remarried an Englishman named John Sketchley who developed a warm affection for young Morton. Sketchley educated the boy and taught him surveying, a useful trade that Morton would practice for the rest of his life—that is, when he wasn't helping to found a new nation.

He entered politics at about age thirty and would serve eighteen terms in various legislatures over the years, on behalf of either Pennsylvania's original royal government or the later state government. Before the war, Morton acted as justice of the peace, then sheriff. Despite his lack of formal training, he served as an associate justice of Pennsylvania's superior court, and toward the end of his days, this simple farmer-surveyor presided over the state government as speaker of the Pennsylvania Assembly.

Serving in Congress beginning in 1774, he was recognized by Benjamin Rush as "a plain farmer." But even Rush had to admit that Morton's previous experience as a justice of the peace had served him well: "[He] was well acquainted with the principles of government, and of public business."

Morton's moment of greatness came as the critical July 2 vote on the Lee Resolution drew near. Besides Morton, Pennsylvania had sent seven men to Congress that season, and they were bitterly divided over the issue of independence. Pennsylvania was largely a Loyalist and Quaker (read: nonviolent) colony. The most vocal delegate, Quaker John Dickinson, had been fighting the independence issue in debate for a month. He felt it was too soon to press for independence, and he insisted that Congress resign itself to diplomacy and reconciliation with Parliament. At the other end of the Pennsylvania spectrum was Benjamin Franklin, who had renounced all allegiance to the king and was ready for independence. Morton, a moderate, was solidly on the fence. He personally supported Lee's resolution, but he knew that the citizens of the region he represented were against it.

A total of four Pennsylvania delegates were leaning toward nay, with only the delegation's senior man, Franklin, and his friend, judge James Wilson, coming down in favor of the resolution. Four against two, with one fence-sitter, does not a revolution make. In an informal vote on July 1, Pennsylvania was solidly against independence, five to two. It looked like the nays had it.

But over the course of one night, the yea-leaning delegates worked their powers of persuasion on the recalcitrant representatives, and by morning the tide had turned. Dickinson and fellow naysayer Robert Morris chose a path that allowed history to take its course without them having to take a stand against it. Come July 2, they simply played hooky from Congress rather than cast their negative votes. That left two delegates, Thomas Willing and Charles Humphreys, casting votes against, and two delegates, Franklin and Wilson, casting votes in favor. The ball landed in Morton's court. The seconds ticked by, and at last the plain Pennsylvania farmer who moonlighted as a judge chose to vote yes, tilting Pennsylvania into the yea column.

Morton, who could now add "signer" to his growing resume, served on a number of committees and presided over the debate on the Articles of Confederation as chairman of the Committee of the Whole, an important but thankless supervisory position. Back home in his district, Morton was unpopular because of what he'd done. A sensitive man, he was said to be deeply affected by his neighbors' ostracism.

About nine months after signing, Morton became sick. His birth and death dates are disputed, but he was probably about fifty-two years old at his death. His historical "first" is a sad one:

He was the first signer of all fifty-six to pass away.

On his deathbed he dictated a message intended for those friends and neighbors angered that he had ignored their wishes by voting for independence. "Tell them," he said, "that they will live to see the hour when they shall acknowledge it to have been the most glorious service I ever rendered to my country."

Those words are engraved on the obelisk over his grave.

John Morton

Benjamin Franklin

THE SIGNER KNOWN THROUGHOUT THE WORLD

BORN: January 17, 1706

DIED: April 17, 1790

AGE AT SIGNING: 70

PROFESSION: Printer, scientist

BURIED: Christ Church Burial Ground, Philadelphia, Pennsylvania

At the time of the Declaration of Independence, Congress was inhabited by two geniuses. One was Thomas Jefferson. The other was Pennsylvania signer Benjamin Franklin, who was a printer, a publisher, a writer, a scientist, a philosopher, an inventor, and a philanthropist all in the same lifetime. Franklin had none of Jefferson's patrician advantages, and yet this self-made man ended his life wealthier, more famous, and more adored than Jefferson. How did this son of a candlemaker pull it off?

Franklin was born in Boston in 1706, the youngest son of Josiah Franklin's seventeen children. His father tried to teach

Franklin his candlemaking trade, but the boy didn't seem interested. Young Ben was then indentured to his half-brother James, a printer. James was a harsh master, doling out many beatings, but Ben excelled in spite of the treatment. He also committed to living so frugally that he could buy his own books, educate himself, and pen secret letters under the pseudonym "Mrs. Silence Dogood." His alter ego was ostensibly a middle-aged widow with strident, often comical opinions about life in the colonies, the fashions of the day, politics, merchant practices, and higher education. Oblivious to the fact that his teenage sibling was the author of these letters, James published them in his newspaper, where they were a great success. Fourteen essays later, the secret was out, and Ben ran away to Philadelphia.

Of all the founding fathers, Benjamin Franklin alone stands out as the cheeky man-child who couldn't resist cracking a joke or tweaking those in power. John Adams described his personality as laced with "infantine simplicity." Historians now say that Franklin's "apprenticeship" with his violent half-brother forever shaped his thinking and actions. As an indentured servant, he was one of only two signers—Pennsylvanian George Taylor being the other—who knew what it was like to be possessed by someone else. It certainly taught him a thing or two about liberty, but if you think that made him less likely to own slaves, think again. Recent scholarship on this question suggests that he owned several throughout his life and never freed them. (Either he sold them or they ran off.) So the puckish persona that Franklin later cultivated does not begin to describe the more complex man who played a profound role in the American Revolution.

In Philadelphia, Franklin's world blossomed. He prospered at the press of another printer, traveled to England, and returned to print a newspaper, the *Pennsylvania Gazette*, and an annual, *Poor Richard's Almanack*. Chock full of maxims such as "A penny saved is a penny earned" and "Early to Bed, and early to rise, makes a Man healthy, wealthy and wise," *Poor Richard's* became absolutely indispensable. Every home in America felt compelled to own at least two books: the Bible and *Poor Richard's*. Farmers craved its planting advice; all colonists wanted its useful calendar. The pamphlet was cheap and written for the ordinary man. Unlike many signers, notably John Adams, who called the populace "rabble," Franklin was sympathetic to simple men, though he was hardly one of them. By age forty-two, he was rich enough to leave his business in the hands of a partner and devote himself to philanthropic work and the building of a new nation.

First he improved Philadelphia life, creating the first American hospital, library, and volunteer fire department. He worked to create the academy that would later grow into the University of Pennsylvania, and he traveled throughout the colonies seeking to better the colonial mail system. As such, Parliament appointed him postmaster general. He also cranked out inventions, including such useful items as the Franklin stove, the lightning rod, and bifocals.

By the way: scientists and historians continue to debate whether he really conducted the famous 1752 kite experiment. Detractors say it's suspicious that Franklin waited four months to publish results of the experiment in his newspaper. And in that account, they point out, Franklin never says that he actually performed the experiment, but that it could be done. Many say he would have died doing the experiment exactly as written. Indeed, a recent episode of the TV show *Mythbusters*—which replicated the experiment and inflicted the sizzling results on a life-sized effigy of Franklin—demonstrated that Ben would have indeed "fried." Do these objections prove anything conclusively? Absolutely not. It's entirely possible that Franklin conducted a safer version of the experiment, and then altered the published details later.

Franklin is so closely associated with Philadelphia and early colonial life that it's somewhat shocking to realize that he lived nearly thirty years of his life in Europe. First, he spent time in London as a young man. Then, as an older gent, he spent ten years, between 1757 and 1770, based primarily in London and another fifteen years—from 1776 to 1785—in France. In England he represented the views of Pennsylvania and was awarded the honorary degrees that conferred upon him the honorific Doctor Franklin. Educated men knew of his kite experiment, and artists painted him as if he were a modern Prometheus, complete with gorgeous hair and lightning bolts in the background.

On his second stay in England, which began in 1765, anti-British furor erupted in the colonies over the Stamp Act, and Franklin was summoned before the House of Commons to explain the American reaction to the policy. The act was later repealed, and he was hailed as a hero back home. But the revolution was just getting started, and Franklin was privileged to witness the British point of view. He tried to explain American sentiment in articles published in local British papers, but his entreaties fell on deaf ears. He sparked a scandal when he leaked damaging antirebel letters penned by the Massachusetts royal governor. In 1774, he was arraigned for disloyalty to the Crown. The solicitor-general ranted for an hour while Franklin stood in silence. Despite the histrionics, Parliament merely stripped him of his postmaster job, which certainly beats being stripped of one's head.

It was time for Franklin to run away once again. He had a new job waiting for him when he returned to the colonies in 1775: Congressman. The shots had already rung out at Lexington, Concord, and Bunker Hill. The colonies were at war. Franklin was pushing seventy. He was the oldest man in Congress and the world's most famous American. He was definitely different from the other delegates in Philadelphia. Sometimes he napped in meetings. Franklin wasn't an orator; he rarely spoke in Congress. His fame rested chiefly on things he had written in private and published in his own media outlets.

But when he wrote, he could be blisteringly savage. When a British friend voted with Parliament against the patriots, Franklin—who had long held a conciliatory view toward relations with the Empire—dashed off a letter, intending to sever their relationship. "You are a Member of Parliament," he wrote in July 1775, "and one of that Majority which has doomed my country to destruction. You have begun to burn our towns, and murder our people. Look upon your hands! They are stained with the blood of your relations! You and I were long friends: You are now my enemy, and I am Yours. B. Franklin." He never sent the letter, but he publicized it openly. It's quoted often as an example of his ability to rage with the best of them.

Early in the war, Congress sent Franklin to Massachusetts to assess Washington's situation. George sent him back with this message: please, for the love of God, send bullets, send troops, send money. Franklin's plan to raise the cash seemed ripped from a copy of *Poor Richard's*; he advocated colony-wide frugality. Throughout the war, he also worked with signer Robert Morris to raise funds. Twice he handed over two sources of his own: the income from his new job as American postmaster general and £3,000 of his own banked savings. The guy didn't fool around.

Later, Congress sent him to Canada with future signers Samuel Chase and Charles Carroll to persuade the Canadians to join their war. The mission failed. When he returned home, he was appointed to the Committee of Five—along with Jefferson, John Adams, Roger Sherman of Connecticut, and Robert R. Livingston of New York—assigned to draft a Declaration of Independence. Jefferson, who was laboring in a room not far from Franklin's own digs, hammered out a first draft, which he sent to the good doctor for comments. Franklin made one now-famous change. He scratched out Jefferson's line, "We hold these truths to be sacred and undeniable," in favor of a sentence that still sends chills down the spine: "We hold these truths to be self-evident."

During the first week of July 1776, when the Pennsylvania delegates were quibbling among themselves over how to come down on the question of independence, Franklin and James Wilson planned to vote yea. Arrayed against them were Charles Humphreys and Thomas Willing, who were definite nays. Two other nay-leaning delegates—Robert Morris and John Dickinson—purposely abstained from the famous July 2 vote. That left John Morton, the fence-sitter, who would have voted nay had it not been for Franklin's persuasion. The 3–2 vote allowed Pennsylvania to squeak by in favor of independence. On August 2, Franklin signed the document with such elaborate flourishes under his name that he gives John Hancock's curlicues a run for their money.

That fall, Franklin hopped a ship on a secret mission to beseech France for troops and funds to fight the war. It was a highly dangerous expedition, but he took along two of his grandsons to keep him company. Seventeen-year-old Temple and seven-year-old Benny were privileged to witness their grandfather's wacky behavior in France. Every morning he lounged around his room naked because he believed that "air baths" were healthful. He wore a ridiculous fur cap to keep his bald scalp warm—and to tweak the French, who he knew imagined Americans as stereotypical frontiersmen. (The fashion became all the rage among the noble ladies of France.) Though he was in his seventies, he incorrigibly flirted with French ladies. He was committed to following his own naughty advice, as found in a letter written while he was still in his thirties, which advised young men to choose older women for mistresses because "they are so grateful!"

Incidentally, his prowess as a ladies' man has been greatly exaggerated. Though he flirted with women of all ages, there's little evidence that he ever conducted an illicit sexual liaison with anyone while his common-law wife, Deborah Read, still lived. (They were together for forty-four years. She died in 1774, when he was in England.) Historians think he sired only three children, two with Deborah and one with another woman, before he "married" Deborah. His illegitimate son was William Franklin, young Temple's father and the royal governor of New Jersey who was ousted and imprisoned by Congress in January 1776. Franklin despaired at his son's decision to side with Britain and refused to help him gain parole. William was released in 1778, and father and son were reconciled toward the end of Ben's life.

When he wasn't captivating older French women, Franklin allowed himself to be fawned over by French philosophers and scientists. After the umpteenth time he saw an image of himself with Voltaire and Rousseau in a gift shop, he wrote to his daughter Sally: "My picture is everywhere, on the lids of snuff boxes, on rings, busts. The numbers sold are incredible. My portrait is a best seller, you have prints, and copies of prints and copies of copies spread everywhere. Your father's face is now as well known as the man in the moon."

As we now know, Franklin charmed the pants off France, which kicked in serious cash and 44,000 troops for the war effort, effectively clinching the war for the Americans. Franklin rode out the war in France. (His finances, unlike those of his fellow signers, actually tripled during the war.) He helped craft the U.S.–Britain peace accord, known as the Treaty of Paris, which he, among others, signed in 1783. Despite the weepy protestations of his French pals, Franklin finally left for home in 1785 because, after all, he was not French. Four years later, the French peasants ran amok; former ally Louis XVI lost his head in 1793.

By then, Franklin was back home helping to shape and sign the U.S. Constitution. In his later years, he wrote his autobiography, which torments high-school students to this day. Did Franklin really intend the book to be so dull, or was he pulling our legs, playing the part of the insufferable self-made man? Where's the sophomoric Ben we know and love?

Finally, in 1790, the printer's apprentice who stood in the presence of five kings and conjured fire from the heavens died at age eighty-four. He is buried in Philadelphia. Ignoring his advice, tourists still fling their hard-earned pennies on his grave.

Benj. Franklin

James Wilson

THE SIGNER WHO WENT BROKE ON SHADY LAND DEALS

BORN: September 14, 1742

DIED: August 21, 1798

AGE AT SIGNING: 33

PROFESSION: Lawyer, judge, land speculator

BURIED: Christ Church Burial Ground, Philadelphia, Pennsylvania

So how does a guy go from signing the Declaration of Independence and coauthoring the Constitution to winding up in a miserable debtor's prison? When it comes to James Wilson, whom some call the second father of the U.S. Constitution, the answer is simple: a lifelong obsession with land speculation caused him to make boneheaded decisions on the bench and brought tragedy and shame into his life. For all his faults, however, he was always one fine lawyer.

Wilson was born in Scotland and studied at not one but three universities before arriving in Philadelphia to seek his fortune. When he soured on a teaching job, he apprenticed at the law firm of John Dickinson, the Quaker who famously refused to vote for independence or sign the Declaration.

Once he was admitted to the bar, Wilson left Philadelphia for Reading, and then Carlisle, Pennsylvania, where he developed a lucrative practice among Scotch Irish settlers. Since many of his cases revolved around land disputes, he absorbed a great deal of privileged information about land parcels and soon succumbed to the lure of land speculation. With borrowed money, he bought land and flipped it for a profit. In time, he acquired a home, a wife named Rachel Bird, and a slave, and he settled into a life he could not have imagined in his homeland.

A lifelong student and thinker, Wilson occasionally found time to lecture on literature and other topics in Philadelphia. He was among the first intellectuals to argue that Parliament had no authority over the colonies and that the colonists should look instead to the king as their link to the Empire. Rebels admired his gift for legal reasoning and welcomed him into the fold. Wilson was probably tickled that incendiary rebels were awed by his logic. He kept coughing up gems for the patriots to use in their cause. Having analyzed Parliament's decision to close the port of Boston, Wilson called for a resolution branding the act unconstitutional. This was a fascinating leap of logic because, under British law, no act of Parliament could ever be considered unconstitutional. But Wilson argued that because colonists didn't have a say in Parliament, this resolution was absolutely unconstitutional. This bit of reasoning was ahead of its time. By presuming to judge whether a piece of legislation was correct, Wilson implied that judges could, and should, second-guess legislators. This concept of "judicial review" would later become a central tenet of the U.S. Constitution.

In Congress, Wilson cut an impressive figure with his six-foot frame, Scottish burr, and dignified expression lurking behind thick, nerdy glasses. Benjamin Rush called him a "profound and accurate scholar" and went on rapturously: "His mind, while he spoke, was one blaze of light."

Politically Wilson was a moderate, though he grew more conservative with each passing year. He was sent to Congress in May 1775. He voted to postpone the vote on the Lee Resolution, but then voted "yes" along with Ben Franklin and John Morton on July 2, throwing the colony of Pennsylvania over into the yea column. But later, when his new state was crafting a constitution that gave power to the citizens, Wilson attacked it. Although he thought that the power of any government rested with the people, he acted like a man without such beliefs. Eventually, such behavior made him unpopular with his constituents, and they yanked him out of Congress in fall 1777.

The greatest urban legend about Wilson is that his home was attacked by the British while he was barricaded inside. The truth is actually more shocking: the British didn't attack his house—the Americans did. In the years following the signing of the Declaration, Wilson transformed himself from a frontier lawyer into a corporate attorney. He switched from being a Whig to a Conservative. He even changed his religion from a traditional Scottish Presbyterian to an Episcopalian. He bought a nice townhouse in Philly, kept buying land, and defended beleaguered Tory merchants in court. Philadelphia's patriots grew to detest him. In fall 1779, when inflation was at an all-time high and food was scarce, a mob of angry citizens and militiamen swarmed Wilson's town-house at Third and Walnut Streets, hoping to tear him to pieces. Wilson and his cronies barricaded themselves inside until another group of militia could rescue them. Some people were injured or killed during the skirmish, and Wilson left town for a while to let emotions cool. The following spring, the legislature pardoned everyone involved in what was sarcastically called the "Fort Wilson" incident.

Wilson returned to public life after the war, when conservatives were in power. At the 1787 convention, he was a major force behind the creation of the U.S. Constitution. James Madison is usually credited as the father of the Constitution, but Wilson, who wrote a draft, is now recognized as the number-two man. He put forth some of the ideas that we now accept as American gospel: that the power of government emanates from the people and that a system of checks and balances is required to ensure that the power invested in leaders cannot be abused. In the end, Wilson was one of the Constitution's thirty-nine signers. Later, he fought to convince Pennsylvanians to ratify the new document, which they did, making it the second state in the union. (Delaware was first.) Then, in what must have seemed like sweet vindication, Wilson was permitted to create a new constitution for Pennsylvania. (Remember: it was his harsh criticism of the original in 1776 that got him yanked from Congress in the first place.)

For all his contributions to America, Wilson expected to be handsomely repaid by being selected as first chief justice of the Supreme Court. He was to be hugely disappointed. He goes down in history as the first justice chosen by President Washington—

but as an associate, rather than chief, justice. That honor went to John Jay. Around the same time, Wilson became the first law professor at the College of Philadelphia, which would someday become part of the University of Pennsylvania.

Despite his brush with mob violence, Wilson never cleaned up his act. He continued to buy land tracts in western New York, Pennsylvania, and Georgia—all on borrowed money. He and his investors had the nutty idea to import immigrants to settle those lands, thereby earning a handsome profit. While on the high court, he was hounded by critics and almost impeached because he tried to promote laws to help—who else?—land speculators.

How could someone so smart be so utterly clueless? When the money stopped flowing, Wilson went belly-up in the land deals. He owed hundreds of thousands of dollars that he couldn't repay. Creditors hounded him to the point that he told a friend he was being "hunted like a wild beast." He even may have used his circuit court duties, which required him to travel around the country hearing cases, as a cover for going on the lam. While still serving on the nation's highest court, he was arrested and served time in debtors' prisons in New Jersey and North Carolina.

These barbaric and illogical prisons, which originated in England and eventually spread to America, were designed to confine a person until they could pay back any monies owed to creditors. Unfortunately, because they were confined, prisoners often had no way of earning a living and became dependent on family, friends, and kind strangers to help extinguish or partially resolve their debts. To make matters worse, prisons often levied fees for staples including food and water and for freedoms such as the ability to sleep in one's cell without being shackled to the wall or floor. So unless a person had the means to pay up, the longer he stayed in a prison, the greater his debt grew. Wilson's confinement was no doubt embarrassing for him, his family, and the United States, and for centuries historians were complicit in covering up the true story.

In 1798, possibly after his release from one of those prisons, he visited Edenton, North Carolina, where his mind finally snapped. He was taken to the home of fellow justice James Iredell. Suffering from acute mental distress, he had to be confined to bed, where he died around the time of his fifty-sixth birthday.

He was buried on a plantation in North Carolina, and his bones did not return to Philadelphia until 1906. Today he's buried outside the walls of Philadelphia's historic Christ Church.

James Wilson

Robert Morris

THE SIGNER WHO FINANCED THE WAR—AND ENDED UP IN DEBTORS' PRISON

BORN: January 31, 1734

DIED: May 8, 1806

AGE AT SIGNING: 42

PROFESSION: Merchant, land speculator

BURIED: Christ Church, Philadelphia, Pennsylvania

Robert Morris is often mentioned alongside George Washington and Benjamin Franklin as one of the three men without whom independence would not have been possible. Washington led the troops, Franklin charmed the French allies, and Morris secured the much-needed moolah. Unfortunately, the man who lived with such wealth, threw all the best parties, knew all the right people, and offered so much financial support for the colonies died in obscure poverty after a three-and-a-half-year stint in debtors' prison.

As signer Benjamin Rush wrote, Morris was "opposed to the time (not the act) of the Declaration of Independence." Morris's many actions, both before and after the signing of the Declaration, certainly support this observation. As an incredibly successful merchant at a leading importing house in Philadelphia, he had already sacrificed much by signing on to boycott the importation of British goods in 1774. Talk about putting your money where your mouth is! And when Morris heard about the Battle of Lexington, he was reportedly so upset that he decided to do all he could for the revolutionary cause. Once he was appointed to Congress, in 1775, he began to put his financial smarts to work, especially through his involvement with the secret committee of commerce, which acquired foreign goods for the military, "paying" for them with in-kind shipments of American goods. In this way, he managed to acquire munitions for the army and beef up naval armaments.

When it came time to vote for independence from Britain, the Pennsylvania delegates were a divided bunch, and despite his patriotism, Morris still didn't believe the time was right. In the "unofficial" vote on July 1, he voted against independence. However, instead of repeating that performance when it counted, Morris absented himself during the official vote on July 2. Presumably he did so to avoid feeling responsible for Pennsylvania being the only state not to approve the measure. But even though the timing of the act wasn't to his liking, Morris was invited to stick around, and he was the only Pennsylvanian who did not vote for independence yet continued to serve in Congress. Morris explained his decision to continue service in a letter a short time later: "I think that an individual who declines the service of his country because its councils are not comfortable to his ideas, makes but a bad subject; a good one will follow if he cannot lead." Morris even went as far as apologizing the following year for not having supported the idea of independence earlier.

Morris signed the Declaration of Independence on August 2, 1776, and apparently found it to be such a thrill that he made a career of signing important documents. He was one of only two signers, along with Roger Sherman of Connecticut, to lend their signatures to all three of the most important documents of the time: the Declaration of Independence, the Articles of Confederation, and the Constitution.

Morris's decision to stay on with the fledgling government was lucky for Congress—and for every American since, really— because without Morris's money smarts (and money, period) Americans today would all be eating chips instead of fries. It's not just that Morris had money of his own; it was that he had a knack for prying it out of the hands of others. A big, hospitable, asthmatic guy and a candid—if not eloquent—speaker, Morris was a natural-born fund-raiser. It's no surprise that he went on to be superintendent of finance under the Articles of Confederation, or that he later played an instrumental role in establishing both the Pennsylvania Bank and the Bank of North America, the country's first government-incorporated bank, which helped collect funds for the ongoing war effort.

Morris came through with cash again and again. His personal credit was much better than Congress's, and he relied on it to get what was needed, often securing loans in his own name. George

Washington sure knew who was buttering his bread. Morris is said to have received a letter from the general written while Washington was camped on the banks of the Delaware. As usual, Washington needed money for the troops, and Morris supposedly got a commitment for the large sum from a wealthy Quaker acquaintance he ran into on the street. A well-funded Washington proceeded to cross the Delaware shortly thereafter and kicked some Hessian butt. Morris's role in supporting Washington during that cold Christmas on the Delaware is uncontested. And there are numerous other stories like it. Every time Washington needed cash, Morris managed to find it, even if it came from his own savings. It is said that Morris gave as much as $1 million of his own money to fund the Yorktown campaign alone.

So where did all of this financial shrewdness and generosity lead him?

Later in life, Morris's luck ran out when he invested a large sum in unsettled land. When the Napoleonic Wars caused immigration to dry up, demand for unsettled land dried up, too, and the value of Morris's land investment dropped severely. In a nutshell, he owed more in mortgage and taxes than the land was worth in a sale. Or, to put it in the terms of a twenty-first-century mortgage crisis, he was upside down on his loans. To pay off his debts, he had to sell everything—all the houses, the properties. There were no federal bailouts at the time, even for the wealthy, so despite all he'd given to fund the revolution Morris was packed off to the Prune Street debtors' prison in Philadelphia. He left not only his family behind, but also a lovely unfinished mansion on Chestnut Street in Philadelphia, designed by none other than Pierre

L'Enfant, the architect who would later plan Washington, D.C. The unfinished house became known as Morris's Folly.

Though Morris's generous contributions to the American Revolution may have caused his fall from grace, few involved in the quest for independence ever forgot that when the government ran out of credit, and when soldiers ran out of food, ammunition, and boots, Morris found the cash. For all Morris had done, President Washington offered him a job as the first Secretary of the Treasury, which Morris declined, suggesting Alexander Hamilton in his place. Washington remained a loyal friend to Morris until the end and even dined with him in debtors' prison. After his release, Morris lived about five more years. He lived out his days in relative obscurity in a small house, dependent on his unbelievably loyal wife (and the small annuity that a friend had secured for her) and their sons. The financier of the American Revolution was seventy-two years old when he died.

George Clymer

THE SIGNER WHOSE HOMES WERE TARGETED BY THE BRITISH

BORN: March 16, 1739

DIED: January 24, 1813

AGE AT SIGNING: 37

PROFESSION: Merchant

BURIED: Friends Meeting House Cemetery, Trenton, New Jersey

George Clymer was a quiet, unassuming businessman who didn't really long for public office. But the new nation could not have survived without men of his keen intelligence—and deep pockets—working behind the scenes.

Clymer was a handsome man with an aquiline nose, wispy hair, and fine, clean features. The son of a sea captain, he was orphaned at an early age and was raised by an aunt and uncle. Luckily for him, his uncle, a buddy of Benjamin Franklin, was a wealthy, cultured merchant. Clymer followed in his uncle's footsteps, devouring every book in the man's library, then raking in the cash from shrewd business deals.

He gave people the impression that he was dispassionate, or even lazy, but his doctor and friend, signer Benjamin Rush, said that nothing could be further from the truth. Behind his polished exterior Clymer was warm, openhearted, and filled with great affection for the patriot cause. He was clearly in favor of breaking with Britain: as early as 1773, when Clymer was about thirty-four years old, he chaired the board that organized the long-overlooked Philadelphia Tea Party, which pressured merchants who were licensed to sell English tea to renounce their posts as royal consignees.

In 1773, Clymer saw some service as captain in a corps of volunteer troops nicknamed the "Silk Stockings," because so many of its members were from well-heeled, blue-blooded families. It's unlikely they saw battle because the war had not yet begun, but they did use their military might to force local merchants to stop selling British tea. Though his military days were short-lived, Clymer distinguished himself with another important wartime service to his new country: fund-raising. He raised money for military supplies of all types—corn, flour, gunpowder, and tenting materials. And he backed the war by exchanging some of his own gold and silver—good, hard cash—for chancy Continental currency that wouldn't have been worth the paper it was printed on if the revolution ended in failure. Clymer's financial support was so integral to the revolutionary cause that he even served as Continental treasurer from 1775 to August 1776.

Clymer was one of the five Pennsylvania delegates—including Benjamin Rush, George Ross, James Smith, and George Taylor— elected to Congress after the July 2 vote. The new congressmen were staunch patriots sent to replace those who had voted against, or refused to vote on, the issue of independence. Most arrived in Congress on July 20 and probably signed the final draft of the document on August 2. For such a virtually unknown signer, Clymer's name pops up a lot in the early congressional committees. He helped deal with food shortages in Philly during the war and even figured out what to do with prisoners of war, specifically the 900 Hessians (German mercenaries) that either surrendered or were captured by Washington's army during the famous crossing-the-Delaware attack on Trenton. Clymer also served on the prestigious committee that drafted the U.S. Constitution. He belongs to an elite group of signers—which includes Roger Sherman of Connecticut; George Read of Delaware; and Benjamin Franklin, Robert Morris, and James Wilson, all of Pennsylvania—who signed both the Declaration of Independence and the Constitution.

Clymer and his family suffered slightly at the hands of the British during the war, but the history books are murky about what actually happened. In September 1777, the Continental Army suffered a defeat in the area of Chadds Ford, Pennsylvania, about 33 miles southwest of Philadelphia, which left the city vulnerable and undefended. Congress was forced to retreat to Lancaster and York, Pennsylvania. Sources say that following that battle, British troops purposely detoured from their march to ransack Clymer's home in Chester County—about an hour outside Philadelphia at the end of the modern-day gaggle of suburbs known as the Main Line—destroying his furniture and stock of "fine liquors." When the British invaded Philadelphia, they purposely sought another of Clymer's homes and began tearing it down, brick by brick, until new intelligence indicated that the house didn't actually belong to Clymer! None of this pillaging, if true, destroyed his ability to earn a living—or to lend money to others. Twenty years after the Declaration was signed, Clymer was back to his old bankrolling ways, bailing out the University of Pennsylvania from possible bankruptcy, founding banks, and so forth.

Clymer died at his home, Summerseat, in Morrisville, Pennsylvania, in 1813. He was seventy-four years old. He is buried in a Quaker cemetery in Trenton, New Jersey, under a modest stone that fails to even mention that he signed the Declaration of Independence.

George Ross

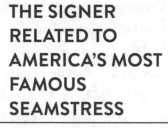

THE SIGNER RELATED TO AMERICA'S MOST FAMOUS SEAMSTRESS

BORN: May 10, 1730

DIED: July 14, 1779

AGE AT SIGNING: 46

PROFESSION: Lawyer

BURIED: Christ Church Burial Ground, Philadelphia, Pennsylvania

As one of the Pennsylvania signers who didn't have to sweat out the vote for independence or wrestle in the Pennsylvania State House over the content of the Declaration of Independence, George Ross is probably best known today for matters of association: one being his relationship to Betsy Ross, the other a matter of chance that left him presiding over a controversial court case that wasn't settled until well after his death.

The most surprising thing about George Ross's turn at John Hancock's table on August 2, 1776, is that he was there at all, for

Ross was a loyal Tory until after his stint in the first Continental Congress of 1774. As a young man, he studied law in Philadelphia and became a successful lawyer in Lancaster, where he served as Crown prosecutor (note the word *crown*), the colonial version of a district attorney. He also worked with the provincial assembly, and despite—or perhaps because of—his standing as a Tory, he was elected to the first Continental Congress. Pennsylvania and most of its delegates were never in much of a rush to split with Britain. Even those who considered themselves patriots or who were appalled by the various acts and taxes that were being handed down by the British were still hoping for reconciliation as late as 1776, as British troops were heading toward New York and Philadelphia.

Around 1775, when the war began, Ross switched his loyalties to the side of the patriots. Maybe some of the rabble-rousers had rubbed off on him, or perhaps it was the shot heard 'round the world. Whatever the catalyst, Ross committed himself fully to the patriots' cause; he even served as a colonel in the Pennsylvania militia. He was elected to the Second Continental Congress in late July and showed up on August 2, 1776, just in time to sign the engrossed document.

Ross left politics in 1777, apparently due to illness, and later became a judge of the admiralty court. There he presided over one of the first legal disputes over where a state's jurisdiction ends and federal rule begins. The case was about prize money awarded for the capture of the British sloop *Active* in 1778. Gideon Olmsted spearheaded the takeover from onboard the vessel. Two other ships moved in, and *Active* was escorted to port. Olmsted was awarded one-fourth of the prize money, with the rest going to

Pennsylvania and the captains of the two privateers. Olmsted felt cheated, so he took his case to Congress, which decided in his favor and told Pennsylvania—via Judge Ross—to pay up. Ross refused to recognize Congress's authority to overturn his and the state's decision. So before the British had even surrendered, and before the Constitution was ever signed, Ross was mired in what was one of the first cases of states' rights. (And Pennsylvania wasn't even a state yet!) The battle raged on for more than *thirty years*, long after Ross was gone, until the Supreme Court finally found on behalf of Olmsted in 1809.

The most popular story about Ross is one that may never have taken place. Ross was the uncle of John Ross, husband of Betsy—the very same Betsy who is touted to schoolchildren as the woman who sewed the first American flag. The story goes that Ross, George Washington, and Robert Morris paid a visit to Betsy at her shop one night and asked her to make a flag for the soon-to-be fledgling country. This is such a lovely story that it's understandable why it has legs. But seriously, Washington? At a time when the Continental Army was busy fighting the British in New York City, it's hard to imagine commander-in-chief George Washington visiting a seamstress in the night to discuss the stylistic virtues of a five-pointed star as opposed to a six-pointed one. Some people erroneously say that Betsy *designed* the flag, which appalls fans of signer Francis Hopkinson, the only person Congress has ever recognized as designer of an American flag (see page 103). Not that Betsy doesn't deserve any credit—she did sew quite a few of the early flags. But we cannot confirm that she sewed the *first* flag.

Overall, George Ross enjoyed a good life and a fine living—and had the gout to prove it. He, along with signers John Hancock, Benjamin Franklin, Benjamin Harrison, and Samuel "Bacon Face" Chase, among others, suffered from the excruciating disease, in which needlelike crystals of uric acid build up in one's joints, causing a painful form of arthritis. Gout typically strikes men, manifesting itself in their big toes. Still something of a scientific mystery, gout is thought to be caused by consumption of rich foods and drinks. Today doctors advise sufferers to shun protein-heavy meals and alcohol. This would have been difficult in colonial times, when salt-cured meats were a sign of one's wealth, and when nearly all citizens drank alcohol, often from childhood, because drinking water was often contaminated. Ben Franklin once wrote a comic dialogue between himself and his gout, in which the ailment mocked him for being lazy and never exercising.

Gout attacks usually last a few days, then subside. Though not considered fatal by modern standards, in colonial times the disease probably exacerbated undiagnosed medical problems. For example, the pain and stress of a gout attack might trigger a heart attack in a patient with heart disease. We don't know what other ailments troubled Ross, but he died after a severe gout attack in 1779, reportedly remarking on his deathbed that he was about to take a "long journey to a cool place where there would be most excellent wines."

Benjamin Rush

THE SIGNER WHO LOVED TO GOSSIP ABOUT OTHER SIGNERS

BORN: January 4, 1746

DIED: April 19, 1813

AGE AT SIGNING: 30

PROFESSION: Physician

BURIED: Christ Church Burial Ground, Philadelphia, Pennsylvania

Remember that kid in school who was smart *and* volunteered after school *and* was active in student government *and* was a member of all the academic clubs *and* had a nice girlfriend and and and . . .

Well, if the Continental Congress operated like high school—and in many ways it did—Benjamin Rush was the kid with the perfect college application, rife with extracurricular activities and do-gooder credits. And just like high school, speaking one's mind against one of the cool kids—in this case, George Washington—can sometimes come back to bite you in the bum. Luckily, Rush's dedication to his patients and his contributions to early American politics far outweighed his loose quill and some questionable medical practices.

After the death of his father when he was a child, Rush was raised by his single mother, who worked in a grocery to secure an education for him. The family lived on a farm outside Philadelphia. Rush studied medicine at home and abroad, then returned to the colonies and embarked on a career that would make him one of the most famous physicians and medical teachers of his time.

Rush was famous for his political activities as well. Though he was not around for the vote on independence—Rush was one of the signers who was elected to Congress after the Declaration of Independence was approved but before it was signed—this youngest signer from Pennsylvania had already been quite active in the prerevolutionary colonies, especially with his pen. He wrote pro-colonist news articles that earned him attention well before he was elected to Congress. A friend of Thomas "Common Sense" Paine, Rush is said to have suggested the title for that famed pamphlet. He had a knack for describing a scene, as is evidenced by this account of the experience of waiting to sign the Declaration, from a letter he wrote to his friend John Adams: "Do you recollect the pensive and awful silence which pervaded the house when we were called up one after another, to the table of the President of Congress to subscribe what was believed by many at that time to be our own death warrants?"

Rush wrote throughout his life about chemistry and medicine, his areas of professional expertise, but also about philosophy, the abolition of slavery, temperance, prison reform, and (here's the part historians love) his fellow signers. It's not that Rush was a gossip, but he was quick—maybe too quick—to share his opinions about others, and he kept extensive notes on his fellow signers and other players in the American Revolution. (He is quoted frequently throughout this book, for his observations provide some much-needed, in-the-trenches insight into the signers themselves.) He detailed who had a sense of humor (George Ross), who had a check-ered past (Samuel Chase), and who was cynical (Abraham Clark).

Rush's eagerness to share his opinions of sometimes got him in trouble. In 1777, his talents as a physician were put to good use in his role as surgeon general of the armies of the Middle Depart-ment. But, true to form, he soon wrote a letter criticizing a superior, Dr. William Shippen, and blaming him for the poor conditions he witnessed. General Washington sent the matter to Congress, which decided in favor of Shippen. Rush resigned his post.

But the writing that had the greatest negative effect on his career came after the Continental Army had been defeated at Brandywine and Germantown. Rush had penned more than one letter criticizing General Washington, but the one he wrote in Jan-uary 1778 to Governor Patrick Henry of Virginia suggesting that the army would be better off with Thomas Conway, Horatio Gates, or Charles Lee as a leader would forever associate Rush with the "Conway Cabal," an episode of political and military back-and-forth that aimed to have Washington replaced as head of the colonial armies. Rush sent the letter anonymously, but when it made its way into Washington's hands, the general recognized the handwriting. Oops. This was the final nail in the coffin of Rush's military career.

In his medical practice, Rush was a strong advocate of using mercury and bloodletting as a treatment for many ailments, practices that earned him a great deal of criticism even in his own lifetime. Despite the fact that bloodletting was a common medical practice since ancient times, he was attacked in print by a newsman, who said Rush's treatments had killed more patients than they saved. Rush sued for libel, but prosecution of the case was repeatedly delayed. The case wasn't settled until late 1799, but George Washington's death—which occurred December 14, 1799, before the libel case was settled—exacerbated Rush's woes. Though Rush did not attend Washington at his deathbed, one of Rush's disciples did, using leeches to suck five to nine pints of blood from poor old George. People blamed Rush's teachings for Washington's death. Rush finally won the lawsuit, but his medical practice suffered in the wake of the case. In 1799, his buddy John Adams lent a helping hand, appointing Rush treasurer of the U.S. Mint, a position he held until his death in 1813.

Despite his embrace of questionable medical techniques, Rush's other humanitarian contributions are beyond question. He treated many patients for no charge, and he established the Philadelphia Dispensary, the first free medical clinic in America. He stayed in Philly during the horrid yellow fever epidemic of 1793, caring for scores of patients each day and seeing the town through the scourge when many doctors had fled. (He even suffered through the affliction himself.) Rush penned America's first textbook about mental ailments, *Medical Inquiries and Observations upon Diseases of the Mind*, and his work in the field of mental health earned him the moniker "The Father of American Psychiatry." (In keeping with his tendency to implement dubious medical treatments, Rush also contributed the "tranquilizing chair" to the psychiatric community, a restraining and sensory-deprivation device that bound limbs and fitted a box with a small opening over patients' heads, "calming" them by restricting blood flow to their brains.) He was even visited in 1803 by Meriwether Lewis (of Lewis and Clark). The legendary explorer would later pack Dr. Rush's antibilious pills, nicknamed "Rush's Thunderbolts," on his great journey west.

Late in his life, Rush was also able to use his skills as a writer to do some good. He is credited with restoring the friendship between John Adams and Thomas Jefferson, whose famous falling out was mended by Rush's own letters as mediator. Long before Sigmund Freud, Rush advocated dream analysis. In 1809, Rush had a quasi-religious dream in which his two old friends had reconciled, enjoyed a rewarding correspondence, and had died "nearly at the same time." Rush shared the details of the dream with both Adams and Jefferson, who eventually did reconcile, exactly as Rush had foretold. Eerily, both died on the same day, July 4, 1826, the fiftieth anniversary of the adoption of the Declaration of Independence.

Despite the libel lawsuit, by the end of his life Rush was regarded as a deeply influential physician and was awarded medals from numerous foreign monarchs. In the end, typhus took his life. Of the American Revolution, he wisely wrote, "All will end well." Of himself, he had an even simpler, yet equally accurate, summation: "He aimed well."

Benjamin Rush

George Taylor

THE SIGNER WHO STARTED OUT AS AN INDENTURED SERVANT

BORN: About 1716

DIED: February 23, 1781

AGE AT SIGNING: About 60

PROFESSION: Merchant, ironmaster

BURIED: First time, at German Evangelical Lutheran Church, then moved to Easton

The best historians agree that nobody knows very much about George Taylor. He is considered the most mysterious of all the signers. But what little is known about him is enough to distinguish this self-made man.

Taylor was born in Ireland and took up the study of medicine. This pursuit didn't last, however, due to a lack of either interest or ability. In any case, the young man, then around twenty, decided to seek his fortune in the colonies and boarded a ship headed to Philadelphia. Like many immigrants, he arrived without a penny in his pocket. According to records, his passage was paid for by a

Mr. Savage, and Taylor was bound to that man and his iron business until his debt was repaid. Taylor shoveled coal to start, and he was eventually promoted to clerk. But even after repaying his debt, the future looked bleak. How much could a penniless indentured servant shoveling coal and working as a clerk expect to improve his lot in life?

Enter fate: Mr. Savage died, and Taylor married his widow, Anne. Now the servant became the master, and Taylor's career as a businessman and ironmaster began to really take off. He built an estate, expanded his ironworks business, and became a member of the assembly in Pennsylvania in 1764. He resigned after several years' service but returned in 1775 and served on several committees, including the one that drafted the instructions for the Pennsylvania delegates who were to attend the Second Continental Congress. Taylor joined the Continental Congress after the legendary vote for independence, but he arrived in time to sign the engrossed document on August 2. From indentured servant to signer of the most significant document in the history of the United States. Only in America . . .

Taylor served in Congress for less than a year and didn't make a huge impression while he was there. As Benjamin Rush succinctly observed: "A respectable country gentleman. Not active in Congress." However, he continued to serve the nation in his own way. In early 1777, he and George Walton (a signer from Georgia) negotiated a peace treaty with the Iroquois at Easton, Pennsylvania. Taylor was also a colonel in the militia, but perhaps his biggest contribution to the revolution came through his ironworks. His furnaces made grapeshot, cannonballs, cannons, and more for the war, but—surprise, surprise—he was poorly compensated for the weapons, if at all. His business suffered as a result. To make matters worse, Loyalist John Galloway owned the lease on Taylor's furnace in Durham, and the new state of Pennsylvania confiscated the forge in 1778, effectively putting Taylor out of business. Taylor moved on to Greenwich, New Jersey, where he leased a forge that he operated until he died.

A year before his death, he returned to Easton. Anne had given him a son and a daughter, and Taylor outlived his son and his wife. For years he had carried on an affair with his housekeeper, Naomi Smith, who reportedly bore him five more children on the side. In the end, documents published by the Presbyterian church and the New York Public Library indicate that Taylor left what money he had to Smith and his grandchildren.

The man who had lived the American dream died in 1781, before America had gained independence. His body was originally buried at the German Evangelical Lutheran Church before being moved years later to the Easton Cemetery, where his grave can be found today.

Geo. Taylor

James Smith

THE SIGNER WHO WAS COY ABOUT HIS AGE

BORN: About 1719

DIED: July 11, 1806

AGE AT SIGNING: About 57

PROFESSION: Lawyer, surveyor, ironmaster

BURIED: First Presbyterian Memorial Gardens, York, Pennsylvania

The Susquehanna River severs the eastern quarter of Pennsylvania from its larger self. Today the river is a mere fact of geography, but in colonial times it was the dividing line between the colony's cultured, prosperous east and the pioneering backwoods. Signer James Smith grew up on the wrong side of this divide, and it shaped him for the rest of his life.

Smith was born in northern Ireland about 1719. His family immigrated to the United States when he was ten years old, and his parents settled on the western side of the Susquehanna. Inhabitants of Pennsylvania's western districts distrusted the inhabitants of the richer, more populous eastern part of the colony, which also held most of the power.

Smith did spend a bit of time east of the Susquehanna; he studied surveying and classical languages at a religious academy in New London, Pennsylvania, about fifty miles southwest of Philadelphia. And after graduation, he lived in Lancaster to learn the law as an apprentice at his brother's law firm. But as soon as he was admitted to the bar, Smith moved back west of the river. He tried to make a go of it in the town of Shippensburg, about forty miles southwest of Harrisburg, but despite knowing two trades—surveying and the law—he just couldn't scrounge up enough clients to earn a decent living. In search of work, he and his family moved to York, about twenty-five miles west of Lancaster, and though he was the only lawyer in town until 1769, he still didn't get much business.

Fed up with earning little in his two chosen professions, he used what money he had to buy a local forge and went into the iron business. This paid the bills, and now he had the time to become fully consumed by politics. Sensing that the colonists would soon be locked in combat, he took it upon himself to recruit a volunteer militia and served as their captain. A staunch Whig, he looked askance at the workings of the Crown and Parliament, and at a political convention in 1774 he called for a boycott of English goods. At various provincial meetings in those few years, he became the voice of Pennsylvania's forgotten western counties, whose residents the law-abiding, Loyalist easterners regarded as uncontrollably "radical." Living up to that stereotype, Smith drafted resolutions calling for independence, a smart military build-up, and the formation of a new subversive government. His

Quaker neighbors shuddered, but it probably didn't surprise them when his constituents sent him to Congress.

There's no doubt that Smith would have voted for independence, but, alas, he wasn't given the chance. He was a member of the crop of new, improved Pennsylvania congressmen—along with George Clymer, Benjamin Rush, George Taylor, and George Ross—elected after the July 2 vote. However, Smith did get to sign the Declaration on August 2.

Smith was a Congressional cut-up. His wit, storytelling prowess, and Irish brogue always entertained the congressmen. During the time that he served in Congress, his business failed because two of his managers had been derelict in their duties, and Smith lost about £5,000. Smith milked even this debacle for a quip. Referring to his employees, he said, "One was a knave, and the other a fool." (Back then, this barb was enough to have your audience rolling in the aisles.) There were, however, two things that Smith never joked about: religion and George Washington. And for some reason, like some vain Broadway diva, he eccentrically refused to tell anyone his age. (His birthdate is a mystery to this day.)

Smith was a deft worker, and he was always willing to lend a hand. In 1777, when the British occupied Philadelphia, Congress retreated first to Lancaster and then to Smith's home base of York. He played the fine host and allowed the Board of War to meet in his law offices. (He probably didn't have clients, anyway.) After Smith left Congress, he took on numerous posts in his fledgling state, including judge, militia general, and advisor during land disputes between Pennsylvania and other states. In 1785, he declined an election to Congress because he felt he was just too old.

Ah, but just how old was he? We'll probably never know, because a fire in his office the year before his death destroyed all the papers that might have helped historians piece together that mystery. Most researchers think he was eighty-six or eighty-seven years old upon his death in 1806, though his grave states that he was ninety-three, which, if true, would put him among the top three oldest signers. The truth has been lost to history.

Once again, James Smith gets the last laugh.

VIII.
Delaware

Caesar Rodney

DELAWARE'S FAMOUS MIDNIGHT RIDER

BORN: October 7, 1728

DIED: June 29, 1784

AGE AT SIGNING: 47

PROFESSION: Planter

BURIED: Christ Episcopal Church, Dover, Delaware

Delaware, the second-smallest state, served as the stage for one of the most dramatic chapters in the signing of the Declaration of Independence. The chief actor? Caesar Rodney, Delaware's answer to Paul Revere.

During the unofficial vote on the Lee Resolution on July 1, it became apparent that Delaware would be one of four colonies presenting serious obstacles to unanimity. The colony had sent three delegates to Philadelphia, but Caesar Rodney, a soldier-statesman, had dashed home to deal with Loyalist uprisings in his neck of the woods. His two colleagues, Thomas McKean and George Read, appeared hopelessly deadlocked. Seeking to break the tie, McKean dispatched a messenger to Rodney's home with a message: get your butt up here!

Rodney, the oldest son of a planter, lived on Byfield, an 800-acre plantation near Dover. From the age of twenty-seven, he'd held an unbroken string of jobs in service to his colony: sheriff, assemblyman, assembly speaker, deed recorder, justice of the peace, and brigadier general in the Delaware militia, among others. (To this day, Delawareans boast that Rodney's litany of public service jobs still stands as a record for any one person in their state.)

In 1776, forty-seven-year-old Rodney was in poor health. He suffered bouts of asthma and the throb of a cancerous lesion that had sprouted on his nose more than ten years earlier and spread to the left side of his face. Philadelphia doctors had excised a portion of the tumor in 1768, but the surgery left a scar that Rodney hid behind a green silk veil. (Many portraits depict him in profile to avoid showing the affected side of his face.) Yet something about his character that struck everyone who knew him. John Adams described him as "the oddest looking man in the world; he is tall, thin and slender as a reed, pale; his face is not bigger than a large apple, yet there is sense and fire, spirit, wit, and humor in his countenance."

McKean's message reached Byfield the night of a terrible storm. Because of his poor condition, Rodney was hardly anyone's first choice to saddle up in the middle of a life-threatening tempest with the fate of his colony's future—and possibly that of all thirteen—in his hands. But Rodney dashed off to his barn and slapped on his spurs. He covered eighty miles in a single night—a journey that typically took two full days. He must have been quite a sight, especially when lightning flashed overhead, revealing the silhouette of a mysterious, veiled man on horseback. What we know for sure is that when Congress met the morning of July 2, an exhausted, sopping-wet, mud-spattered Rodney was there, casting the vote that threw Delaware 2-to-1 in favor of independence.

The story of Rodney's midnight ride is the stuff of legend, and it is recounted in children's picture books to this day. The details of his journey are still debated by historians. Did this sickly man really accomplish what was normally a two-day's trip in one night? Isn't his dramatic ride just a little too dramatic? Some argue that Rodney must have traveled by carriage at least part of the way.

We may never know the details, but at least part of the famous story is true. In 1989, Christie's auction house sold a remarkable letter Rodney wrote to his brother on July 4, 1776—the only existing letter from that date in which a signer actually refers to the Declaration of Independence. The letter, now in a collection at the University of Virginia, reads in part:

> *I arrived in Congress (tho detained by thunder and rain) time enough to give my voice in the matter of Independence. . . . We have now got through with the whole of the declaration and ordered it to be printed so that you will soon have the pleasure of seeing it.*

Despite the fact that citizens of Dover celebrated the Declaration's signing with a massive turtle feast, the colony was still home to staunch Loyalists who lashed out at Rodney and McKean in future elections. Rodney's courageous ride did not earn him a seat at Delaware's Constitutional Convention or first legislature. Nonplussed, he turned his attention to military affairs and recruited local troops to support General Washington during the New Jersey campaign in the winter of 1776. Rodney briefly commanded the post at Trenton after the victory, when Washington had moved on to Morristown. The following fall, 1777, when the Brits invaded Delaware, Brigadier General Rodney defended the colony with his troops and shortly thereafter was appointed by McKean, then acting governor, as major general of the local militia.

Rodney's health grew progressively worse as he aged, but he was too dedicated to his work to give in to illness, saying, "I am determined to persevere." From 1778 to 1781, he served as acting and then full governor (in those days, the title was "president") of Delaware, despite sometimes being so sick that he couldn't travel to assembly meetings. In these instances, the assembly came to him, and meetings were held at his home.

The man who'd done so much for Delaware's independence didn't live to see it become the first to ratify the U.S. Constitution. Rodney died in June 1784, at age fifty-six, leaving no wife or children. (Among the signers, he and North Carolina's Joseph Hewes were the only lifelong bachelors.) Rodney was buried at Byfield, then reinterred one hundred years later under a more elegant marker in Dover. And though his fellow Delawareans didn't shower him with accolades for ensuring the success of the Declaration at the time, Rodney enjoys full hero status there today. A giant statue of him astride a horse stands in Rodney Square in Wilmington, and schools, dormitories, and, fittingly, a half marathon are named in his honor. A handsome statue of him represents Delaware in the Capitol's Statuary Hall in Washington, D.C., and the Delaware state quarter shows Rodney galloping away.

Casar Rodney

George Read

THE ONLY SIGNER WHO VOTED AGAINST INDEPENDENCE

BORN: September 18, 1733

DIED: September 21, 1798

AGE AT SIGNING: 43

PROFESSION: Lawyer

BURIED: Immanuel Episcopal Churchyard, New Castle, Delaware

What can you say about a guy who voted against independence when the chips were down but then signed on with the program a month later? Well, if the guy is George Read, you say he was a man committed to voting his conscience, a conscience that believed in independence . . . just not so soon.

Read was a moralist. He was a man of reason. He also behaved as did many of the ardent supporters of separation from Britain. He opposed British taxes. He supported the Non-Importation Agreements, a boycott of British goods. And when those naughty Bostonians were slapped with the Boston Port Bill by the British, as punishment for their little impromptu tea party, Read's county reportedly raised $900 to help them get back on their feet. Super-rebel Samuel Adams even wrote Read a thank-you note.

Delaware sent Read to Congress in 1774, along with Thomas McKean and Caesar Rodney. Read naturally hit it off with Pennsylvania's John Dickinson, a powerful speaker who opposed independence. During those first days of July 1776, Dickinson often found himself in the ring with John Adams. Dickinson argued that independence was a premature step, and Adams claimed the time was already past. Cautious Read was in Dickinson's camp.

Read wasn't the only delegate to vote against the resolution on July 2, but as one of three representatives from Delaware and the only holdout among them, his vote took on special importance. Delaware representative Caesar Rodney was tending to business at home and wasn't expected to be in Philadelphia for the vote on July 2, which meant that Read and pro-independence delegate Thomas McKean were deadlocked. If the vote proceeded without Rodney, Delaware's vote would have been thrown out. The Declaration would not have passed unanimously. But when McKean discovered Read's intended vote, he sent a courier to Rodney, who pulled an all-nighter on horseback to make the eighty-mile journey from Dover to Philadelphia to cast his tie-breaking vote. If Rodney hadn't made his midnight ride, Read's "nay" vote would have seriously weakened Congress's position.

While some in Congress abstained from the vote on Lee's resolution (therefore allowing it to pass), and others voted against independence and later refused to add their signature to the

Declaration, Read did what may seem quite odd, even unthinkable, for a vote of such life-threatening and treasonous importance: he voted against independence on July 2, but then stuck around and signed the document anyway. Does he deserve to be remembered as a flip-flopper, voting one way but then later going along with the cool kids?

Read's grandson later published *The Life and Correspondence of George Read*, in which he defended his grandfather and others who did not vote for independence. The younger Read pointed out that in hindsight it is all well and good to say that voting for independence was a great idea, but that taking on the world's most powerful empire with no real army to speak of and limited funding and resources must have seemed much different at the time. When presented that way, it's easy to see why some people showed more than a little trepidation.

Once the resolution passed, Read accepted the results as the desire of his fellow men and did his part for the fight against the British, whom he never favored in the first place. Read was not only happy to sign on, he immediately supported the cause in a big way, raising money for supplies and troops and even taking up arms in the militia. As Pennsylvania delegate Joseph Galloway remarked, when Read signed, he "did so with a rope about his neck." Read himself did not disagree. "I know the risk, and am prepared for all consequences," he replied.

Though Read did not lose property or possessions in the war, he did experience at least one very close call. In 1777, when Delaware's governor John McKinly was taken prisoner by the British, Read, then vice president of the state, was summoned to

Wilmington to take over. He left Philadelphia with his wife and children and started down the Jersey shore of the Delaware River. They attempted to cross the river at Salem, New Jersey, when their boat not so conveniently grounded within sight of a British ship. Troops were on Read's boat like white on rice, but Read managed to escape by playing the role of a traveling country gentleman who was simply heading home with his family. (Some accounts say that Read removed any identifying marks or documents from his possessions before the British pulled up.) In any case, the clueless British took him at his word and politely helped the patriot and his family to shore.

Read held a variety of positions and appointments in his life and went on to participate in the Federal Convention of 1787, which drafted the Constitution. He is one of only six people who signed both the Declaration of Independence and the Constitution. In fact, he was having such a good time that he signed the Constitution twice: once for himself and once for his old friend John Dickinson, who had to leave the historic proceedings early for unknown reasons (presumably for something of grave importance—perhaps a wig-fitting?). A strong Federalist, Read's efforts in support of the Constitution led Delaware to become the first state to ratify the document. This of course resulted in Delaware's nickname, the one it proudly bears on hundreds of thousands of exhaust-stained license plates to this day: "The First State."

Thomas McKean

THE SIGNER WHO WAITED FIVE YEARS TO SIGN

BORN: March 19, 1735

DIED: June 24, 1817

AGE AT SIGNING: 41–46

PROFESSION: Lawyer

BURIED: Laurel Hill Cemetery, Philadelphia, Pennsylvania

Thomas McKean of Delaware had a ridiculously long resume, even when compared to type-A overachievers such as John Adams, Thomas Jefferson, Robert Morris, and Caesar Rodney. McKean is the only signer who was governor of one state (Delaware) while serving as chief justice of another (Pennsylvania). But there was one item on his curriculum vitae that he wanted his fellow Americans to remember: that he truly was a signer of the Declaration of Independence.

McKean was the very last man to sign the Declaration. Just before he died at age eighty-three, he insisted that he had signed the document in the presence of Congress sometime in 1776. But since the official version of the Declaration released by Congress in January 1777 did not include his signature, McKean is believed to have signed sometime after that date. In fact, some historians believe McKean may not have signed until 1781, a full five years after everyone else. Ironically, the reason for McKean's tardiness is linked to his impressive list of credentials: the guy was just too darn busy.

McKean began pumping up his resume at an early age. As a young man, he studied law at a cousin's office in Delaware and practiced in both Delaware and New Jersey. Next, he racked up a laundry list of jobs in Delaware's colonial government: Sheriff. Militia captain. Notary officer. He was a loan office trustee in one county, a customs collector and a judge in another, and the deputy attorney general in yet another. Eventually, he ascended the ranks of the Delaware legislature, becoming speaker of the lower house, where he was vocal during the angry days of the Stamp Act. Later, despite moving with his wife to Pennsylvania in 1774, McKean was sent to Congress, where he would serve for eight of the nine subsequent years. It may sound strange that Delaware would send to Congress a man who actually lived in Philadelphia, but before 1776, Pennsylvania and Delaware were politically linked.

McKean was hard to miss, with his six-foot height and ramrod-stiff posture. He was known to use humor in some of his court cases but was otherwise a serious man with a prickly disposition. Quick to anger, he could be cold, tactless, and vain. He was fond of wearing his hat at a rakish angle and carrying a gold-capped cane.

McKean is remembered mostly for the role he played in Caesar Rodney's famous midnight ride. On July 1, 1776, McKean discovered that his fellow Delaware delegate George Read was planning not to vote for independence the next day. McKean knew that Delaware's third delegate, Caesar Rodney, would vote for independence, but Rodney was eighty-six miles away in Delaware. McKean sent a courier to summon him, and the following morning he met the disheveled Rodney at the door of the statehouse. Skinny, sickly Rodney had ridden all night to reach Philadelphia. The two men walked inside and voted yea. Read voted nay. The 2–1 vote tilted Delaware in favor of independence.

That same month, shortly after casting his vote, McKean led the Pennsylvania Associators, a militia group, to assist George Washington during his defense of New York City. On August 2, when so many of the other delegates were signing the Declaration, Colonel McKean was at war.

McKean's life continued its rapid pace in the years that followed. When he wasn't dodging cannonballs on the battlefield, he was either slaving away on legislation for Delaware or running from the British with his wife and eleven children. When the British captured the rebel governor of Delaware, McKean assumed the post until fellow signer George Read arrived from Philadelphia to take over. Chagrined, the British put McKean on their hit list. In 1779, McKean told John Adams that he was being "hunted like a fox by the enemy—compelled to move my family five times in a few months, and at last fixed them in a little log house on the banks of the Susquehanna . . . and they were soon obliged to move again on account of the incursions of the Indians."

In 1781, McKean served as president of Congress under the Articles of Confederation, holding the oft-forgotten title of

President of the United States in Congress Assembled. Some historians think that McKean signed the Declaration during this period, becoming the last to add his signature to the document, though of course his own statements are at odds with this theory. He later served three terms as Pennsylvania's governor, beginning in 1799. His administrations were stormy, to put it mildly. McKean demanded that people do things his way, censured opponents, and appointed friends and relatives to lofty posts. He antagonized critics, who then tried to have him impeached.

As he aged, McKean was occasionally asked by government recordkeepers, journalists, or historians to explain his role in the signing of the Declaration. Though his name was officially on the document, other sources conflicted with the notion that McKean had signed around the same time as everyone else. So McKean took on yet another role: Declaration Debunker. At age sixty-two, he wrote letters seeking to clarify the record. You can imagine the colonel getting increasingly peeved. It may have seemed tacky to toot his own horn, but what choice did he have? "Modesty should not rob any man of his just honor," he would write, "when by that honor his modesty cannot be offended." Further complicating McKean's case was the fact that Thomas Jefferson, Ben Franklin, and John Adams all referred to July 4 as the day of the signing, cementing that date in the national psyche.

McKean died a wealthy man in 1817 and was buried not in Delaware, but in Philadelphia. In a posthumously published statement, McKean in effect said: no one signed the Declaration on July 4, 1776. If you do your homework, you'll discover that at least seven of the signers were not even elected to Congress until after

July 4, 1776. He seemed miffed that supporting Congressional documents had omitted his contribution for so long, though, as we've said, no one buys his own assertion that he signed sometime in 1776. When did he sign? Sometime between 1777 and 1781 is anyone's best guess.

Shockingly, in 1819, seventy-six-year-old Jefferson dismissed McKean's claims that no one signed on the fourth, writing "Mr. McKean was very old, and his memory much decayed when he gave his statement." Ironically, historians today say they are more persuaded by McKean's statement than by Jefferson's. The colonel, though not fully vindicated, would have at least approved of that.

IX.
Maryland

Charles Carroll of Carrollton

THE LAST SIGNER TO DIE

BORN: September 19, 1737

DIED: November 14, 1832

AGE AT SIGNING: 38

PROFESSION: Merchant, planter

BURIED: Doughoregan Manor Chapel, Ellicott City, Maryland

Charles Carroll had a lot to lose by signing on with the patriotic cause. As if the British weren't enough of a problem, religious intolerance almost prevented him from practicing law and serving in public office. However, he overcame these hurdles with smarts and charm and suffered no losses at the hands of the enemy during the war. He ended his very long life as he had begun it—as perhaps the richest man in America.

Carroll was born in Carroll Mansion in Annapolis, Maryland, the child of a wealthy tobacco planter. Sharing your name with a mansion is always a good start to life, yet despite all the family's go-to-hell money—and they could have afforded to send the entire colony to hell, had they wanted—life for the Catholic Carrolls was still quite difficult.

Being Catholic was a big problem in those days, even in Maryland, a colony originally planned by George Calvert, first Lord Baltimore, and founded by his son, Cecilius, as a Catholic colony named after a Catholic queen. Unfortunately, the reigning religion in the colonies had already turned, thanks to the Crown, to Protestantism—so the same kind of persecution that Catholics had suffered in Ireland dogged them in the colonies. Catholics couldn't vote, hold public office, teach, practice law, and so on.

Despite these hardships, the Carrolls' fortune provided them with opportunities other Catholics lacked. Young Charles attended a secret school with Jesuit instructors before his family wisely sent him off to complete his studies in Catholic-friendly France, followed by a short stint at law school in England.

He returned to America in 1765, all grown up and loaded with aristocratic charm. He danced, he fenced, he spoke French, and he had 10,000 acres all his own—he really was quite a catch. In 1768 he married his cousin (back then, it was pretty hard not to) Mary Darnall, and the two began a family that eventually included seven children. Carroll soon had his family, Carrollton Manor, an Annapolis residence, and Doughoregan Manor to look after. In an effort not to be confused with one of the gaggle of Charles Carrolls running around (his father and a Congressman cousin among them), he added "of Carrollton" to the end of his signature. It did have a nice, if repetitive, ring to it.

Though he couldn't practice law, one thing he could do was

write. In the early 1770s, the proprietary governor of Maryland decided to raise everyone's taxes so that government officials could get a raise. Government taxing the people for its own pay increase remains an unpopular practice today, but imagine this happening on the heels of the Stamp Act and all the other Intolerable Acts perpetrated by Britain at the time. The colonists were more than a little unhappy at the prospect of handing the government even more of their money. However, there did appear to be at least one supporter of the tax. A Daniel Dulany wrote to the *Maryland Gazette* in defense of the government's position, using the not-so-creatively named characters "First Citizen" and "Second Citizen" to illustrate his point. First Citizen argued against the tax, while Second Citizen—Dulany's voice—supported the measure. About a month or so later, Charles Carroll wrote a response under the name "First Citizen" to express the patriots' point of view. A duel of the pens was on. Everyone read their literary skirmishes. When people learned that "First Citizen" was Charles Carroll, his notoriety and popularity soared. The Catholic was in.

Carroll supported nonimportation agreements (a boycott of British goods), attended Maryland's first revolutionary convention, and was on the committees of correspondence and safety. He was asked by his fellow conventioneers to be a delegate to the first Continental Congress, but he declined, probably thinking that his beliefs would be a problem on the larger stage. However, he still went to Philadelphia as an unofficial member of the Maryland delegation.

In 1776, though Carroll was still not a member of Congress, his talents and abilities were requested on Benjamin Franklin and

Samuel Chase's mission to persuade French-speaking, Catholic-heavy Canada to lend support to the colonies in the war. This was quite a responsibility for someone who was "along for the ride" in Philadelphia. But as John Adams explained, "He speaks their language as easily as ours; and what is perhaps of more Consequence than all the rest. He was educated in the Roman Catholic Religion. . . . In the Cause of American Liberty his . . . Fortitude and Perseverance have been so conspicuous that he is said to be marked out for peculiar Vengeance by the Friends of the Administration; but he continues to hazard his all, his immense Fortune, the largest in America, and his life." Carroll and his cousin John (who went on to become the first Catholic bishop of the United States) joined the delegation to Canada, but the gang soon discovered that it was going to take more than *parlez-vous* and a few Hail Marys to win the support of the Canucks. America's first diplomatic mission to another country went the way of the dodo; it never took flight and was eventually dead and forgotten.

Around this time, Congress had also decided to postpone the vote on Lee's resolution until July 2. Carroll and Maryland delegate Samuel Chase knew that Maryland had yet to give her delegates the go-ahead to vote for independence, so they headed down to Annapolis and worked the convention. Thanks in part to Carroll's influence, Maryland did indeed change position, and the delegates were free to vote for independence.

Carroll was not in Philadelphia for the vote for independence on July 2. He was chosen to represent Maryland in Congress on July 4, 1776, the same day the Declaration of Independence was adopted. He reported for duty on July 18, in plenty of time to sign the engrossed document in August. In addition to being the only Catholic signer, he was also the only one to pen more than just his name, signing "Charles Carroll of Carrollton." One of the most popular stories from that historic day describes Carroll stepping up to Hancock's table to sign. After finishing, he was making his way back to his seat when a fellow congressman commented, "There go a few millions."

The man who didn't have to work a day in his silver-spoon-fed life stayed very busy. He was a member of the Maryland state senate for years, and in 1776 he helped draft the Maryland constitution and served on the board of war. He also served on the committee that visited General Washington at Valley Forge. As a big supporter of George, Carroll helped break the Conway Cabal that sought to relieve Washington of his duties as commander of the armies. In 1778, Carroll was asked to act as president of Congress, but he declined. He was elected to, but did not attend, the federal Constitutional Convention, though he did help rally support for the ratification of that historic document in Maryland. And from 1789 to 1792, he served as one of Maryland's first two United States senators.

He spent the rest of his life—and we're still forty years away from the end of it—close to home. After all, at this point he had more than 70,000 acres to keep track of, and all the chores that went along with owning that much land. He also owned hundreds of slaves, possibly more than anyone in the United States. Later in life, Carroll changed his mind about slavery and manumitted some of his own before he died. However, like other slave-owning signers who began to question the practice, he still kept some to run his plantation. In 1789, he also introduced a bill for the "gradual abolition of slavery" to the state senate, where it was promptly ignored.

Carroll was still going strong throughout his seventies and eighties, but people around him were dropping like flies. His father, his wife, his son—he outlived them all. The War of 1812 came and went. He invested in canal systems. He had land in Pennsylvania and even more in New York. He also served on the first board of directors of the Baltimore and Ohio Railroad and laid its cornerstone in a ceremony at the age of ninety-one. He was known to take daily horseback rides into his nineties.

By 1826, only three of the legendary fifty-six signers were still alive: Thomas Jefferson, John Adams, and Charles Carroll. Jefferson and Adams died on July 4, 1826, the fiftieth anniversary of the adoption of the Declaration. Adams's last words—not knowing his old friend and rival had already kicked it a few hours earlier—were "Thomas Jefferson survives." What he *should* have said was, "Charles Carroll survives." And for six more years, Carroll did just that, serving as a kind of a living monument to the American Revolution. People would stop by to see him, pay him homage, and perhaps check his pulse. He wintered his last several years with his daughter in Baltimore, which is where he died at the age of ninety-five. And then there were none.

Charles Carroll of Carrollton

Samuel Chase

THE SIGNER BETTER REMEMBERED AS "OLD BACON FACE"

BORN: April 17, 1741

DIED: June 19, 1811

AGE AT SIGNING: 35

PROFESSION: Lawyer

BURIED: Old St. Paul's Cemetery, Baltimore, Maryland

So how does anyone end up with a nickname like "Old Bacon Face"? It helps to have an abrasive personality. From virtually the moment he entered public life, Samuel Chase was the sort of man who always managed to say something that rubbed people the wrong way. He had a gift for oratory that allowed him to crush an opponent with just the right turn of phrase. To protest the Stamp Act in 1765, Chase, the leader of the Annapolis Sons of Liberty, broke into the office where the stamps were stored, destroyed them, and burned the tax collector in effigy. After this demonstration, the Loyalist mayor denounced him in the local paper. In an article printed in the same paper, Chase condemned his critics as nothing more than "despicable tools of power." He railed: "I admit, gentlemen, that I was one of those who committed to the flames, in effigy, the Stamp distributor of this province, and who openly disputed the Parliamentary right to tax the colonies, while you skulked in your houses. . . . Others of you meanly grumbled in your corners and not daring to speak your sentiments."

It's strange to think of the twenty-five-year-old writer of these words as the son of a mild-mannered preacher, but that was indeed Chase's background. His mother, Matilda, died shortly after childbirth, and Chase's father, Thomas, moved from the country to take over St. Paul's Church in the "village" of Baltimore.

Physically, the boy grew to be a big man—more than six feet tall and solid—who knew how to use his body to intimidate his rhetorical opponents. After studying law in Annapolis, Chase became a member of the Maryland Assembly and quickly gained a reputation as a virulent anti-Brit. He opposed virtually any decree made by the royal governor. His fraidy-cat colleagues realized what a gift they'd been handed: here was a man unafraid to speak his mind, even when he was picking on the most powerful people in the land. (This was where the "Bacon Face" name originated, thanks to his reddish-brown complexion.) Soon he was sent to the First and Second Continental Congresses.

In 1776, Chase, Benjamin Franklin, and Marylander Charles Carroll traveled to Canada on an unsuccessful mission to seek that nation's military support. When they returned to Philly, Chase was horrified to learn that Maryland's legislators back home still hadn't decided how to act on the matter of independence. Chase and Carroll dashed back to Annapolis and drummed up support for the upcoming vote. Thanks in part to Chase's persuasive tongue, his pivotal colony gave its thumbs-up, and Maryland's delegates in Philadelphia received instructions to vote in favor of independence.

Chase was in Maryland on July 2, 1776, and therefore was not among those who participated in the historic vote. However, a famous myth, repeated in several history books, has him pulling a Caesar Rodney (see page 163), riding 150 miles to Philly in just two days to cast his vote. Where did this lie come from? Believe it not, it was Congress's fault. Because officials altered the Congressional record to reflect that all fifty-six signers signed on July 4, 1776—in accordance with the grand myth that we all grew up with—they introduced anachronisms that could only be explained by ridiculous leaps of logic. Later historians knew Chase was in Maryland in late June/early July, helping his state write its own declaration of independence. And yet, here was the official record saying he signed the Declaration on July 4 in Philadelphia.

So what really happened? The truth, as you'd expect, is somewhat prosaic. Chase's wife was sick, and therefore he did not return to Congress until mid-July. We know that not being able to vote for independence galled him, because on July 5, when he still had not heard that Congress had voted for independence, he wrote to John Adams: "I hope ere this time the decisive blow is struck. Oppression, inhumanity, and perfidy have compelled us to it. Blessed be men who effect the work! I envy you. How shall I transmit to posterity that I gave my assent?"

His chance to go on the record came on August 2, when he signed. It may have been his finest moment. From then on, though he always managed to secure numerous, impressive positions in the new nation, his overbearing manner always seemed to win him new enemies. He was forced to leave Congress in 1778, when newspapers claimed he'd used insider information to profit from the wartime flour market. Discredited, he went back to Maryland, where he made a series of bad investments, went broke, and devoted himself to building his legal practice and restoring his finances.

He married twice, fathered a gaggle of kids, and served as a judge in Baltimore for many years. When Washington became president, he rewarded Chase for his wartime service by appointing him to the Supreme Court of the United States. Here, too, Chase's mouth got him in trouble. Some observers objected to the way he bullied defendants and their lawyers from the bench. Occasionally, too, he launched into partisan diatribes. After the turn of the century, when Jefferson was president, Chase was frequently heard unabashedly bad-mouthing the Saint of Monticello's policies. "Under Jefferson," he said, "our republican Constitution will sink to Mobocracy, the worst of all possible governments." The House of Representatives voted to impeach him, but the case got bogged down in the Senate. The crux of the trial hung on the prosecutors' assertion that Chase had ruled unfairly in several cases because of his political biases.

Cooler heads prevailed. In March 1805, Chase was acquitted, and his impeachment trial set the precedent—which stands to this day—that judges cannot be impeached, sued, or removed from office because of their beliefs. Remarkably, Chase goes down in history as the only Supreme Court justice to be impeached.

Chase grew fatter with age, his face no doubt getting more bacon-y. Gout finally forced his retirement. He died at age seventy and was buried in what is now Old St. Paul's Cemetery in Baltimore. You'll find him there today, not far from the tomb of Francis Scott Key, the author of "The Star-Spangled Banner."

Samuel Chase

William Paca

THE SIGNER WHO DARED TO ACKNOWLEDGE HIS ILLEGITIMATE CHILD

BORN: October 31, 1740

DIED: October 13, 1799

AGE AT SIGNING: 35

PROFESSION: Lawyer, planter

BURIED: Wye Plantation family plot, Wye Island, Maryland

As a young man, William Paca was good friends with future signer Samuel "Bacon Face" Chase. As young law clerks in Annapolis, the two young men trolled the public houses, raged about the wrongs the colonies had suffered at the hands of the British, and then, suitably tanked, hit the streets and burned various figures in effigy. Paca probably picked up the bar tab.

Paca's parents were wealthy Maryland planters. They ensured that he received a proper education, grounded in the classics. He studied "away" at Philadelphia, then "away" at London at the prestigious Inner Temple, and eventually he returned home to practice at an Annapolis law firm.

That's where he met Chase and another future signer, Thomas Stone. All three were studying law or clerking at Annapolis firms. Paca married a young Annapolis belle while in his twenties, but that didn't end his days of carousing with Chase. The two were inseparable and incorrigible, though Chase was more of a vocal firebrand and the quieter Paca preferred to pen devastating letters. In one public demonstration, the two staged a mock execution of an unpopular law that the royal governor had just passed. They inscribed the law on a sheet of paper, marched it to a mock gallows, strung it up as if they were hanging it by the neck, waited until it was "dead," cut it down, lay it in a coffin, and buried it under the gallows. A ship parked in Chesapeake Bay fired a small cannon to cap off the ceremony. Paca owned the ship, and he no doubt settled the bar tab wherever the protestors partied afterward.

Later, the duo objected to a tax paid by citizens to support the Church of England. Chase's father was a clergyman, but he and Paca both thought it was wrong for the government to collect a tax that benefited a single religion. The letters and articles Paca and Chase wrote and published branded them as rebels in the eyes of Tories and as patriots in the eyes of Whigs. The legal eagles had their first big test case when a political friend was arrested and fined for refusing to pay the tax. The jury found for their client, awarded him £60 in damages, and Paca and Chase were hailed as heroes. Their adversary in the courtroom was friend and fellow signer Thomas Stone.

Paca gained a reputation as the leader of this band of rebels and was soon elected to both the First and Second Continental Congresses, where he remained a delegate until 1779. His memory has been sullied by the gossipy signer Benjamin Rush, who wrote that Paca was "a good-tempered worthy man with a sound understanding that he was too indolent to exercise. And hence his reputation in public life was less than his talents." To be fair to Paca, Rush was no great admirer of Chase and probably painted Paca with the same brush. But Paca never experienced any of the political scandals that dogged Chase. Even Rush had to admit that Paca was "beloved and respected" and considered a "sincere patriot and honest man."

Maryland was one of the fence-sitting colonies that almost didn't vote for independence. The Annapolis Convention—a rebel-led political body—had not authorized its three delegates in Philadelphia to take such an action. Paca and Thomas Stone were in Philly waiting for word from Annapolis as Congress crept closer to the vote. Chase and another signer, Charles Carroll—who had not yet been elected to Congress—were in Annapolis, trying to persuade the Convention to give its assent, which it finally did. When their instructions arrived, Paca and Stone voted in favor of the Lee Resolution. (They were joined by a third Maryland delegate, John Rogers, who voted but left Congress before signing.) Chase and Carroll were still in Maryland on July 2, but they signed the Declaration in August with most of the other representatives.

Paca's memory lives on mostly in association with contributions he made on the state level. He spent thousands of his (family's) money supplying Maryland's troops. He helped the Annapolis Convention create a new state constitution and later served as a state senator. He then rose from a chief justice to Maryland's third governor, serving until 1785. He cared deeply about veterans of the war and during his term worked to provide assistance for them. When Congress was debating the new Constitution, Paca supported it at the Convention and drew up a list of amendments that would serve as one of the foundations for the Bill of Rights.

Paca lost many of his loved ones and was said to be lonely toward the end of his days. His first wife died ten years after their marriage, and two of their three children also died during his lifetime. He remarried, only to have his second wife die three years later, followed by their only child together, who died at age two. He had one child out of wedlock with a free black woman. Paca's choice to acknowledge and raise their child, Hester—sending her to all the finest schools—raised more than a few eyebrows.

Paca died at age fifty-eight at his posh estate on Maryland's eastern shore. He is buried on the grounds of his old plantation on Wye Island, on the Chesapeake.

Thomas Stone

THE SIGNER WHO DIED OF A BROKEN HEART

BORN: About 1743

DIED: October 5, 1787

AGE AT SIGNING: About 33

PROFESSION: Lawyer, planter

BURIED: Thomas Stone National Historic Site, Port Tobacco, Maryland

Signing the Declaration of Independence was certainly the most audacious act of this quiet, unassuming man's short life, especially since at the time he was one of the few stalwart conservatives in Congress.

Thomas Stone grew up on a plantation, became a lawyer, and married Margaret Brown, a union that netted him a tidy sum via her dowry. The money enabled the pair to buy land near Port Tobacco, and in 1771 Stone built Habre-de-Venture, which would remain his home for the rest of his life. He and his wife had three children. Whether it was love at first sight or merely an arranged marriage, the two became deeply attached as the years passed.

Stone began his public service the way many professional men of the day did: he was on the county committee of correspondence. These committees were charged with establishing communication with the other colonies, which allowed the nascent states to work together on common goals. Though he supported the colonists' cause, he was not an advocate of war and violence. In 1774, he received some early—but not necessarily positive—public exposure in the developing battle between the patriots and the motherland when he acted as a prosecutor in a case against a man who had refused to pay the poll tax being collected to support the Anglican clergy. By that time, taxes had long been a touchy subject for the colonists, and supporting the Crown's position in this matter did not boost Stone's popularity among the patriots. The defense team was made up of William Paca, Thomas Johnson, and Samuel Chase, all of whom would later be at Congress when Stone took his seat. He lost the case.

Despite this setback, he was elected to go to the Continental Congress later that year. Maryland was hesitant about independence, hoping, as many did, that everyone could resolve their disagreements without a drawn-out, bloody war. When Stone took his seat in 1775, he supported the somewhat head-in-the-sand approach to dealing with England shared by many fellow Marylanders. He was quiet in Congress, but when the time came to vote on Lee's resolution, he went along with everyone else. Other noted conservative signers—e.g. Braxton and Rutledge—did the same.

Perhaps Stone's most significant contribution was his role on the committee that drafted the Articles of Confederation, which were not approved until November 1777. He remained in Congress until 1778, and he continued his duties as a member of the state senate. In 1783 he was again elected to the Continental Congress, and the following year he was even acting president briefly—not bad for someone who barely said "boo" and kept hoping that the colonies and Great Britain would kiss and make up.

After representing Maryland at the Mount Vernon Conference in 1785, Stone was elected to attend the Constitutional Convention in 1787, an event that coincided with one of the great tragedies of his life. Unfortunately his beloved wife was yet another victim of a smallpox inoculation gone bad. During revolutionary times, this inoculation involved plucking pus from an existing smallpox victim and transferring the goop to an incision under the skin of an individual who had not yet been exposed to the deadly disease. The newly infected person typically came down with a mild case of smallpox and was kept in quarantine until he or she recovered, immune from then on. The treatment worked, but it wasn't exactly foolproof. There was always the chance you might die, go blind, or pass it on.

Stone's wife became ill after her inoculation in 1777 and lived in worsening health for a decade, never recovering. The Constitutional Convention began in May 1787; Stone's wife died in June. He never recovered from her death. Grief-stricken and depressed, Stone gave up his law practice and planned a trip to England. While waiting for his ship in Alexandria, Virginia, he suddenly collapsed and died, just four months after losing his wife. He was only about forty-four years old.

Thos Stone

x.

Virginia

Carter Braxton

THE SIGNER WHO HAD EIGHTEEN CHILDREN

BORN: September 10, 1736

DIED: October 10, 1797

AGE AT SIGNING: 39

PROFESSION: Planter, businessman

BURIED: Chericoke House family plot, King William County, Virginia

Carter Braxton was the most reluctant and conservative of all Virginia's signers. Some say he was the most reluctant signer among the whole lot. Perhaps the fact that he possessed vast wealth and had eighteen children to support—more than any other signer—had something to do with it. When you've got a lot to lose, it's hard to take risks.

The son of a rich Virginia planter, Braxton was rolling in cash, land, and slaves. His mother, Mary, was the daughter of Robert "King" Carter, so nicknamed because of his fabulous wealth. (He owned forty-two plantations.) Mary died after Braxton's birth, and his father died when the boy was in his teens. Raised by family friends, Braxton married shortly after he graduated from the College of William and Mary. He became even wealthier thanks to property he received as part of his marriage package, though his wife, Judith, died in 1757 after the birth of their second child, just two years after their wedding.

After Judith's death, Braxton dashed off to England for business, hoping to clear his head. When he returned in the 1760s, he was steeped in British sentiment. He settled into a comfortable life in the colonies, occupying at least two plantation homes, first Elsing Green and later Chericoke, with his first two children, his second wife, Elizabeth Corbin, and the sixteen children they had together.

In the 1760s, Braxton tried to invest money in the burgeoning slave trade. "I am told there is a great Traid carried on from Rhode Island to Guinea for Negroes," he wrote in 1763 to brothers John and Moses Brown of Providence, "and I should be glad to enter into Partnership with some Gentlemen for a Voyage or two and have [the slaves] sent here where I believe they sell as well as any where."

Later that year, he advised the Browns on which "products" would bring the best price: "The Gold Coast slaves are esteemed the most valuable and sell best. The prices of Negroes keep up amazingly. They have sold from £30 to £35 sterling a head clear of duty all this summer[.] I should not doubt of rendering such a sale if the Negroes were well and came early." The Browns, whose family fortune would eventually help found that Ivy League bastion, Brown University, spurned Braxton's offer and instead financed a disastrous slave voyage on their own.

To our modern eyes and ears, Braxton's words are deeply and morally offensive. But the unfortunate reality is that other signers probably spoke about slavery in similar terms. If their spoken words were not reported, or their letters on the topic have not survived, then those men come off as somehow more saintly than Braxton. Despicable as they are, Braxton's surviving letters help historians shed light on the unsavory world of slave trading.

With his power and wealth, it's no surprise that Braxton sat in Virginia's House of Burgesses, the elected body sanctioned by the king and the royal governor in Williamsburg. These were tense times in Virginia. Egged on by radical Patrick Henry, the Burgesses rebelled against the Stamp Act, saying that Britain had no right to tax the colonies. In fact, they claimed that only Burgesses could tax Virginians. Braxton supported these so-called Virginia Resolves. At this point in his political career, he did not favor breaking with Britain. Like a lot of wealthy planters, he just didn't want the Crown picking his pockets.

The friction between the royal governor and Virginia's patriots mounted after the battles of Lexington and Concord. News of the rebellion caused such panic in the governor that he ordered the seizure of all the gunpowder in the Williamsburg magazine. When Patrick Henry learned of the confiscation, he flipped his wig and marched into town with a gang of militiamen, demanding either the gunpowder's return or full payment for it. Braxton defused the situation, speaking to the governor's representative on Henry's behalf to hammer out an accord. Ultimately, the governor paid up, and the patriots emerged victorious. Two things ensured Braxton's success at defusing the hostile situation. First, he straddled two different political worlds at the same time. He was a member of the landowning aristocracy and loved Britain, but was on cordial terms with all radicals in the House of Burgesses. Second, the governor's representative was Richard Corbin, Braxton's father-in-law.

Braxton's entrenchment in the world of Virginia's power elite is the chief reason he was sent to the Continental Congress in 1775. Some people said that Virginians were originally so appalled at the idea of independence that they sent a man who was sure to counteract the views of "violent" radicals such as John and Samuel Adams. Braxton distrusted New Englanders and early on derided the cause, saying, "Independence is in truth a delusive bait." He felt that America could never declare independence because the colonies were simply "too defenseless" without a strong navy. But Virginia had "violents" of its own—men such as Patrick Henry—who would ultimately sway opinion in that colony.

As late as July 1, Braxton opposed independence. Yet come July 2, he voted with all the others. Why the change of heart? Perhaps his fellow Virginians Thomas Jefferson, the Lee brothers, and his own rebel cousins, Benjamin Harrison and Thomas Nelson, twisted his arm. Or perhaps he was too politic to buck the trend. Regardless of Braxton's change of heart, it does not seem that his fellow Virginians ever fully trusted his patriotic leanings. When he wrote a draft of a new government for Virginia, it was rejected because it was simply too aristocratic. (Braxton was uncomfortable with the idea of democracy.) After signing the Declaration, the radicals held sway in Congress and back home. Braxton was not reelected to Congress, though he did find a home in the Virginia legislature for the rest of his life.

In his defense, Braxton did help the American cause throughout the war. He bought supplies for the troops, lent a fortune (£25,000) to the fledgling government, and—slaves still on the brain—floated the idea that enslaved men should fight in the war. The idea was shot down due to resistance in the South, though many slaves did run away to join the British, who promised freedom if they fought.

Braxton is often described as having lost everything at the hands of the British, but this claim is somewhat exaggerated. He had partnered with the British government, investing heavily in sailing vessels, but the ships and their cargoes were seized during the war, and Braxton's investments were doomed. Was this because he was a signer? Doubtful. A war was on, and ships and cargo were darn handy no matter who owned them. And though his plantations were probably attacked and damaged during the war, his homes were not destroyed. In fact, they're still standing today.

Besides the money he lost on the ships, Braxton was never repaid the funds he lent the United States government. It wasn't long before creditors came calling. An old myth has him dying "in rags," but it's more likely that he was plagued by lawsuits and just too broke to pay. After the war, he downsized to a less expensive residence, where he died, probably of a stroke, at age sixty-one. A fine memorial to the Braxton family stands in a Richmond cemetery, though the signer was buried at Chericoke in an unmarked grave. The exact location of his plot has never been found.

Carter Braxton

Benjamin Harrison

THE SIGNER WHO PLAYED FALSTAFF TO CONGRESS

BORN: April 7, 1726

DIED: April 24, 1791

AGE AT SIGNING: About 50

PROFESSION: Planter

BURIED: Berkeley Plantation, Charles City, Virginia

With his huge frame and red face, corpulent Benjamin Harrison has been dubbed the Falstaff of Congress. The tales of his Congressional hijinks always seem to revolve around the same gag—his size—and may be more legend than truth. A prudent historian might ignore such tales entirely, but they shed wonderful light on the machinations of the Congressional chamber. And besides, they're great fun.

Harrison came from an incredibly wealthy family of planters from Berkeley Plantation, west of Williamsburg along the James

River. He was a grandson of a man referred to as "King" Carter, which made him the cousin of signers Carter Braxton and Thomas Nelson, also of Virginia. He was the fifth person of the same name in his family, so historians sometimes refer to him as Benjamin Harrison V, though that's not how he signed the Declaration of Independence. Harrison went to school at the College of William and Mary but left to become the man of the house when his father, Benjamin IV, and two of his siblings were killed in a lightning storm. Ben V did an excellent job running the estate and built the family business to include eight plantations and a thriving shipping business.

Harrison was elected to the House of Burgesses while younger than twenty years old, but that genteel body overlooked his youth in favor of his pedigree. His political beliefs were generally moderate to conservative, but he was sympathetic to the patriots' cause, beginning with their objections to the Stamp Act. Between 1773 and 1776, he was heavily involved in all the business of the revolution: attending conventions, writing letters, and so on. He was sent to the First Continental Congress, where he bunked in a Philadelphia flat with none other than George Washington. At the Second Continental Congress, as emotions were heating up along the seaboard, he joked that he had resolved to attend this critical session even if he had to walk from Virginia to get there. The thought of a fleshy, 240-pound aristocrat hoofing it to Philly surely gave the other attendees a good chuckle.

Of all the Virginia delegates, which included Thomas Jefferson, the Lee brothers, Thomas Nelson, George Wythe, and Carter Braxton, Harrison was probably the second-most conservative, slightly to the left of Braxton. As a result, his motives were impugned by John Adams, who called Harrison "an indolent, luxurious, heavy gentleman, of no use in Congress or committee, but a great embarrassment to both."

Puritanical New Englanders had long squabbled with the flashy Southerners, but Adams was being grossly unfair to Harrison, who admirably served on three major committees—state, war, and navy. Benjamin Rush, hailing from Pennsylvania, had a more balanced, mid-Atlantic opinion of Harrison's talents. "He had strong state prejudices and was very hostile to the leading characters from the New England states," Rush admits. "In private life he preferred pleasure and convivial company to business of all kinds. . . . He was upon the whole a useful member of Congress, sincerely devoted to the welfare of his country."

Once, the story goes, when the members needed to select a new president of Congress, some liked Hancock for the job, but Hancock pooh-poohed the notion. Six-foot-four Harrison crossed the room in a bound, physically lifted the smaller Hancock, and plopped him down in the president's chair. "We shall show Mother Britain how little we care for her," Harrison reportedly said, "by making a Massachusetts man our president, whom she has excluded from pardon by public proclamation." (At this point in history, Hancock and Samuel Adams were reportedly wanted for treason by the Crown.) All laughed but John Adams, who was jealous of the attention being shown to Hancock, his rival.

Later, Harrison was elected as chair of the Committee of the Whole, a crucial role in which he presided over important congressional debates. John Adams was not in favor of Harrison's elevation, probably because he suspected Harrison was too moderate to lead the debaters forward to independence. But Harrison surprised them all. Each day, Hancock yielded the president's chair to Harrison to preside over the morning's debate. In the afternoon, Hancock resumed his seat as president, and Harrison issued his committee's report. In this capacity, Harrison chaired two major debates: the July 2 vote on independence and the July 4 adoption of the Declaration. He later headed debates on the Articles of Confederation as well.

Harrison signed the Declaration with the majority on August 2. According to a popular story, on that day he reportedly made light of the fact that they were all signing a treasonous document. Turning to tiny Elbridge Gerry of Massachusetts, he allegedly joked that they would face vastly different fates at the gallows if America did not win the war. "With me it will be over in a minute," he quipped. "But you, you'll be dancing on air an hour after I'm gone."

Again, another fat joke from the king of self-deprecation. The only problem with the story is that it couldn't have occurred on August 2, because Gerry wasn't in Philadelphia that day. So either Harrison said it to Gerry on another occasion, or he said it to another shrimpy congressman, or he didn't say it at all. We'll never know.

Harrison left Congress in 1778 and became a speaker in the Virginia legislature. In 1781, British Loyalists, led by Benedict Arnold, swept through Richmond and camped near Berkeley Plantation. The extent of the damage they caused is unclear, but some sources claim they occupied Berkeley and burned some of

Harrison's possessions, including paintings from his walls; they also may have burned his shipyard and seized the cargo. Harrison and his family fled inland to escape the trouble, but none of this, if true, was particularly devastating to his family's health, wealth, or standing. Indeed, the house is still intact and open for tourists.

After the war, Harrison continued to make his voice heard on the important issues of the day. He went on record insisting that the Bill of Rights must be included before the ratification of the U.S. Constitution rather than after, so strongly did he feel about those guarantees of American rights. He served three terms as the fifth governor of Virginia.

Congress's jovial fat man departed this earth in a manner befitting his size. One night in 1791, he died after an attack of gout. He was sixty-five. Interestingly, his descendants include two of the least remarkable presidents in United States history: William Henry Harrison (who died after one month in office) and Benjamin Harrison (whose most notable achievement may have been cutting his own children out of his will).

Thomas Jefferson

THE SIGNER WHO WROTE THE DECLARATION

BORN: April 13, 1743

DIED: July 4, 1826

AGE AT SIGNING: 33

PROFESSION: Planter, lawyer, violinist, inventor, botanist, architect

BURIED: Monticello, Virginia

What can we say about Thomas Jefferson? He was a lifelong student of, well, almost everything. The man loved learning. He was a diplomat and an architect. He played violin. He invented the first swivel chair. He designed his own massive home—and his own tomb. He grew and ate tomatoes at a time when they were considered poisonous and planted grapevines when everyone thought American soil was unsuitable for vineyards. He was obsessed with climate data and carried measuring tools in his pockets at all times. He tinkered with keys and locks, dabbled in archaeology, and read voraciously. He doubled the size of America in 1803 with the Louisiana Purchase. We could get lost forever in a list of his fascinating achievements and factoids. But here we will focus largely on how he breathed life into the Declaration of Independence.

Born and raised at Shadwell, a plantation in what is now Albemarle County, Virginia, Jefferson came from a privileged family. His father died when Jefferson was in his teens and left him a considerable estate and slaves. As a young man, Jefferson enjoyed an excellent private education, attended the College of William and Mary, and went on to study law under the incomparable teacher, fellow signer, and father figure, George Wythe. "No man ever left behind him a character more venerated than George Wythe," Jefferson once wrote. Wythe had an enormous and lasting influence on Jefferson, who even started a biography on his great teacher (though he never finished).

Jefferson began building his home at Monticello in 1768, but it was not completed until after he was president. In 1772, he married Martha Wayles Skelton, and her dowry added considerably to his already sizable fortune. Tall, thin, athletic, red-headed, and shy as can be, Jefferson was graced with an education and position in society that made him a natural for public service, even if his personality did not. He entered Virginia's House of Burgesses at age twenty-six. From the start, he got more attention as a writer rather than as a speaker. He was elected to the Continental Congress in 1775 and arrived in May 1776, just when things were getting revved up.

Congress chose a Committee of Five—Benjamin Franklin, John Adams, Robert R. Livingston, Roger Sherman, and Jefferson—to oversee the writing of the Declaration. Livingston and

Sherman contributed little to the actual writing of the document; indeed, Livingston, a New York delegate, was most likely chosen to ward off objections from the on-the-fence New Yorkers. And though the resolution calling for independence had been presented in Congress by Richard Henry Lee, Jefferson was chosen to draft the Declaration because he had fewer enemies than Lee—and because he was acknowledged by all to be an excellent writer. So Jefferson holed up in the small, second-floor parlor he rented on Market Street, bent over the portable writing desk he had invented, and scribbled away, quill feathers flying. Jefferson knew that the Declaration would be read aloud to countless American citizens, so he paid special attention to the sounds and cadences of his prose. (In one of the surviving drafts, you can actually see marks above the words where he analyzed the rhythms of his sentences.)

Jefferson once said that the Declaration of Independence was an "expression of the American mind"—not just his. He took inspiration from the philosopher John Locke and from the ongoing discourse (read: fights) that he witnessed in Congress. His language was clearly inspired by Virginia's George Mason, who had written the Virginia Declaration of Rights. (Mason's line "all men are born equally free and independent" should ring a few bells.) This should not detract from Jefferson's flowing prose, however. The Declaration was tweaked before it was presented to Congress, primarily by Franklin and Adams. (Jefferson: "We hold these truths to be sacred and undeniable." Franklin: "We hold these truths to be self-evident.") The committee submitted the Declaration to Congress on June 28, just days before the scheduled vote.

Once the vote for independence passed, the delegates began

revisions on Jefferson's baby. Editing by committee is never a good idea, and getting fifty or so men to agree on every word in a single document is damned near impossible. It must have been a painful process, but Jefferson, still not much of a speaker, kept his mouth shut. Franklin consoled Jefferson as the most important thing he had written in his thirty-three years was run through the shredder, and the congressmen were still arguing days later on July 4. "The debate seemed as though it would run on interminably," Jefferson wrote. The Pennsylvania State House (now called Independence Hall) was hot, humid, and infiltrated with horseflies. Some eighty-six changes later, everyone agreed on the language. John Hancock and secretary of Congress Charles Thomson signed, and off to the printer it went. Some historians argue that Jefferson accompanied the document to the printer and proofread each of the drafts as it came off the press.

In September, Jefferson returned to Virginia, where he served on the legislature. The greatest achievement of this period was probably his Virginia Statute for Religious Freedom, which took seven years to pass. He served as governor for two years during the war, but he didn't make a very good impression. In 1781, the British invaded Virginia and the legislature pulled out of Richmond. Jefferson resigned shortly afterward, suggesting that he be replaced by someone with a strong military background. Fellow signer General Thomas Nelson Jr. took over. The following year Jefferson lost his wife, Martha; they had been together roughly a decade, and he was crushed by her death. In 1783, he returned to Congress and within a year was off to France, where he served as minister for five years.

For a guy who probably would have preferred to be home reading and working in his garden, Jefferson was just too darn smart and capable in too many fields for anyone to let him off the hook. President Washington made him the country's first secretary of state, which put him in close quarters with his nemesis and archrival, Secretary of the Treasury Alexander Hamilton. Jefferson believed in the ideals of republicanism—that all men could govern themselves—and despised Hamilton's federalist stance, which held that a strong, central government would guarantee a strong nation. Their feud would run well until Jefferson won the 1800 election on the Democratic-Republican ticket and Hamilton took a bullet in the gut from Aaron Burr, Jefferson's vice president.

Before his gig as secretary of state was up, Jefferson resigned, planning to head home to Monticello. But after losing the presidential election to John Adams by a mere three electoral votes, the law of the day stipulated that he would become vice president. After serving for four years under his former friend—their political views had diverged and their friendship was on the skids—Jefferson was elected as the country's third president, rendering Adams a dreaded one-term president. Adams did what a lot of presidents still do to this day: he got as many of his cronies into positions of power (as judges, etc.) as he could before vacating his post, and then he coldly split before Jefferson's inauguration. None of this helped their already strained friendship, and they would not speak or correspond with each other for nearly a decade. Jefferson served two terms, accomplishing the Louisiana Purchase and sending Lewis and Clark on their famous expedition.

Finally, in 1809, he returned to Monticello, wrote letters, and entertained people, which was a burden on his already overextended finances. He also dedicated a huge amount of time to the founding of the University of Virginia. Thanks to signer Dr. Benjamin Rush, Jefferson and Adams eventually reconciled in their old age and once again spent a lot of time doing what they loved—writing long, flowery letters back and forth. In one such missive, dated January 21, 1812, Jefferson wrote his long-lost pal: "A letter from you calls up recollections very dear to my mind. It carries me back to the times when, beset with difficulties and dangers, we were fellow laborers in the same cause, struggling for what is most valuable to man, his right of self-government."

Jefferson's legacy is long and varied. Of the six children he had with Martha, only two girls reached adulthood and one died before her father. He is also believed to have fathered at least one and possibly all six of the children of Sally Hemings, his slave. As early as his tenure in the Burgesses, he argued for the emancipation of slaves, but he didn't free the vast majority of his own during his lifetime. Jefferson did free two slaves (both with the last name Hemings), and three more left Monticello with Jefferson's "tacit consent." (They were also all named Hemings.) Five others were freed in his will, three of whom shared the last name of—you guessed it—Hemings.

He never freed Sally, but Jefferson's surviving daughter permitted Sally to leave shortly after his death. In a letter to Edward Bancroft in 1788, Jefferson wrote, "As far as I can judge from the experiments which have been made to give liberty to, or rather abandon, persons whose habits have been formed in slavery is like abandoning children." More than one hundred slaves were sold at the estate sale after his death.

Jefferson ended his life functionally bankrupt. Problems from years of neglecting his finances were exacerbated by the economy (ain't that always the way?), and he was barely getting by. His fate was sealed when a friend welched on a very large loan, forcing Jefferson to sell his library to the government. Lucky for the rest of the country, those books became the seed of the Library of Congress. Jefferson died on July 4, 1826, just hours before his friend John Adams.

The world remembers Jefferson for myriad accomplishments, but he wished to have only three things on his tombstone: author of the Declaration of Independence (good choice, Tom), author of the Virginia Statute for Religious Freedom, and founder of the University of Virginia. Apparently, in his eyes, the whole President of the United States thing was small potatoes by comparison.

Richard Henry Lee

THE SIX-FINGERED SIGNER

BORN: January 20, 1732 (or, according to the Lee family Bible, January 1733)

DIED: June 19, 1794

AGE AT SIGNING: 44

PROFESSION: Planter, merchant

BURIED: Burnt House Fields, Lee Family Estate, Coles Point, Virginia

Richard Henry Lee was the older, flashier, and more outspoken of the two Lee brothers who signed the Declaration. In his long career in public service, his most notable act was the one that got the nutty ball of independence rolling: he put forth in Congress the legendary resolution for separation from Great Britain, which led to the creation of the Declaration of Independence.

Richard Henry Lee was born into a well-known family and followed the same path as most of its members: he was educated in England, returned home, started a family, and entered public life. Though the Lees were quite renowned and one of the most established families in Virginia, Richard didn't have an excessive amount of money. In a sense, he was just too busy to focus on earning any.

Lee began his public service as a justice of peace, and by 1758 he joined four of his brothers in the House of Burgesses, Virginia's legislative body. Early on, he was quick to point out that the British constitution guaranteed some of the rights that the folks in the colonies wanted to protect and that the colonists should not be denied them just because they lived an ocean away. He opposed the slave trade from early on as well, and though his opinions didn't have much of an effect on the institution, it was said that he favored "so heavy a duty on the importation of slaves, as effectually to put an end to that iniquitous and disgraceful traffic within the colony of Virginia."

Lee was soon associating with all the rowdy kids, including the rebellious Patrick Henry, with whom he hit it off early. Together they formed the core of the Virginia Sons of Liberty; they drew up nonimportation agreements, organized boycotts of British goods, and were all-around outspoken, patriotic fellows.

In 1767, Lee told Pennsylvania's John Dickinson that it would be a good idea for the colonies to find a way to communicate with one another, but it still took five years before the colonies put the system into action. Massachusetts asserts that the so-called committees of correspondence were their idea; Virginia says no, it was theirs. Their letters claiming credit probably passed each other on horseback somewhere in New Jersey.

In any case, by 1773 Lee, Henry, and Thomas Jefferson had started the Virginia committee of correspondence and asked other colonies to do the same. Virginia protested the closing of Boston Harbor by the British—a surprising show of solidarity with their

Yankee cohorts. When both Lee and Henry arrived at the First Continental Congress, the Massachusetts clique immediately embraced their fiery ways, and Lee became fast friends with Samuel Adams. And there Lee's reputation as a speaker began to grow. Sometimes nicknamed "Cicero" for his oratorical prowess, Lee was described by John Adams as one of Congress's "great orators." His speeches were accentuated by the visual flourish caused by the movement of a black silk scarf he tied around one of his hands. His motivation for wearing the scarf was not mere theatrics—a hunting accident had blown off all his fingers except his thumb.

Lee put his knack for stringing words together to excellent use when he introduced his now-famous resolution for independence on June 7, 1776. He was in favor of cutting off relations with Britain, working to form foreign alliances (Bonjour, France!) and preparing a plan for confederation. His resolution was seconded by feisty John Adams so quickly that it almost knocked the powder out of Lee's wig. The resolution read:

> Resolved, That these United Colonies are, and of right ought to be, free and independent States; that they are absolved from all allegiance to the British Crown, and that all political connection between them and the State of Great Britain is, and ought to be, totally dissolved.

According to procedure, the guy who made the resolution should have been able to write any supporting documents. But for a variety of reasons, it was decided that Thomas Jefferson should be primarily responsible for penning the Declaration of Independence. Some say choosing Jefferson was solely a political move on John Adams's part; others believe Lee needed to attend to personal affairs in Virginia. In any case, Lee was not even on the Committee of Five charged with drafting the document. It appears as though he wasn't bothered by the exclusion. He even complimented Jefferson on the document, saying that, "the Thing is in its nature so good, that no Cookery can spoil the Dish for the palates of Freemen."

Oddly, Lee didn't stick around Philadelphia for long after the committee was appointed to draft the Declaration. In fact, he didn't even make it back to Congress in time to vote on his own resolution—though he did eventually find time to sign the Declaration that his resolution inspired.

Later in life Lee lost popularity at home. He foolishly sided with his wrongheaded brother Arthur when the latter accused Congressman Silas Deane—one of America's representatives in France—of improper conduct in the securing of munitions there. History fingers Arthur as the kook in this episode and Richard as having perhaps defended him without knowing the real deal. Whatever the reason, Richard's poor judgment and blind loyalty kept him from earning enough votes to return to Congress in 1777. His brother Francis Lightfoot Lee resigned his own delegate position in protest, as did other supporters. Shortly thereafter Richard was asked to fill a new vacancy, and he—and his brother Francis—returned to Congress to serve until 1779.

During the war, Lee fought in the Virginia militia and had his horse shot out from under him during a battle. In 1784 he returned to Congress and served as its president from 1784 to 1785. He left once more in 1789. During that time, he declined election to the Constitutional Convention and instead led the opposition against the document. The idea of a strong federal government bugged him, and he was not alone in the sentiment. After all, the colonies had just squirmed out from under one suffocating government that quashed people's rights, and he certainly didn't want to be party to the birth of another. But his stance was not all bad news for the fledgling nation—he led the charge to incorporate the Bill of Rights, which, of course, the founders did. Lee even served as one of his state's first two U.S. senators after Virginia became a state. He resigned in 1792, for health reasons. (Lee was yet another signer who suffered from gout; see page 149.) He died just two years later. His grave is in the Lee family cemetery.

Richard Henry Lee

Francis Lightfoot Lee

THE SIGNER WHO LIVED IN HIS BROTHER'S SHADOW

BORN: October 14, 1734

DIED: January 11, 1797

AGE AT SIGNING: 41

PROFESSION: Planter

BURIED: Mount Airy, Tayloe Family Estate, Warsaw, Virginia

A member of one of the most reputable and respected families of the time, Francis Lightfoot Lee is best remembered as the younger brother of fellow signer Richard Henry Lee. Francis was always overshadowed by big bro's flowery speeches and remarkable career. Not that the younger Lee wasn't a revolutionary—far from it. In fact, he was often considered to be more of a patriot than big brother Richard.

Francis Lightfoot Lee was born at Stratford Hall in Virginia. (Years later, another, more famous man with the surname Lee would be born at Stratford Hall, but he would fight against the union his ancestors had worked to create.) There were eleven children in the Lee family, and Francis lost both his parents before he was an adult. Francis and Richard, who is believed to have been about two years older, entered public life in 1758. Francis was trustee for the village of Leesburg, and he soon moved on to the House of Burgesses, Virginia's elected body, where he would serve until being elected to Congress in 1775.

It would be unfair to say that politically the two men were of one mind. They often acted together, but on occasion stood alone. If there was one way in which Francis distinguished himself from Richard, it's that he was probably more outwardly patriotic. Benjamin Rush wrote of Francis, "He was brother to Richard Henry Lee, but possessed I thought a more acute and correct mind." Early on, the Stamp Act really raised Francis's dander. From the moment Parliament passed that law, if there was a protest, an assembly, or even a slightly perturbed gathering at a plantation barbecue, Francis was there.

Francis helped form the Virginia committee of correspondence in 1773, signed the call for a Virginia convention, and then moved on to join the Continental Congress in 1775, where he served until 1779. The two brothers had originally been very shy, but where Richard overcame this defect, Francis clung to it. In Congress, he was quiet and reserved, a stark contrast to his brother, who had transformed himself with patient training to become one of the most accomplished orators of the time. Francis quietly labored off the congressional floor, on the board of war and the military and marine committees. Of course Francis voted for independence. How could he not? His brother put forth the storied resolution! He signed the declaration on August 2, with the bulk of the signers.

Family can be a blessing and a curse. The Lees were plagued by the twisted machinations of their addled brother Arthur, who had been sent to France—along with Benjamin Franklin and one Silas Deane—to drum up support for the American cause. Arthur insisted that Deane had profited personally from sales of supplies granted by the French, and Richard supported his claims. (It was later revealed that Deane was an honest man, albeit a lousy bookkeeper.) In 1777, Richard, who suffered a long bout of declining popularity because of the Deane affair, was not reelected to Congress. Francis—loyal brother that he was—resigned in protest, along with some of their supporters. The ploy worked, and when a new opening in the Virginia delegation arose, Richard was sent back to Congress. Luckily for Francis and his compatriots, the House ignored their resignations, so they were all able to continue as delegates.

Despite Francis's quiet nature, he held several important Congressional positions. He worked on the committee to draft the Articles of Confederation, and when that document was later replaced by the Constitution, he stood as a staunch supporter of the new legislation, opposing the position of his brother. This was one of the rare times that the two brothers differed politically. Richard had long been suspicious of handing over too much power to a central government. Remarkably, Virginia followed little brother Lee's lead in this respect, ratifying the Constitution in 1788, making it the tenth state in the new nation.

Francis Lightfoot Lee resigned in 1779 and left Congress for a four-year stint in the Virginia state senate before retiring from public life completely. He finished his life quietly, spending time with his wife, Rebecca, at Menokin, their Virginia home, which today is a tourist site. The couple had no children, and they died within a short time of each other from a suspected bout of pleurisy. (In other words, they caught a bad cold.)

The legendary Mark Twain, writing about Francis in 1877, may have captured the essence of the quieter Lee brother the best: "This man's life-work was so inconspicuous, that his name would be wholly forgotten, but for one thing—he signed the Declaration of Independence. Yet his life was a most useful and worthy one. It was a good and profitable voyage, though it left no phosphorescent splendors in its wake. . . . In short, Francis Lightfoot Lee was a gentleman—a word which meant a great deal in his day, though it means nothing whatever in ours."

Thomas Nelson Jr.

THE SIGNER WHO ORDERED TROOPS TO FIRE ON HIS OWN HOME

BORN: December 26, 1738

DIED: January 4, 1789

AGE AT SIGNING: 37

PROFESSION: Planter, merchant

BURIED: Grace Episcopal Churchyard, Yorktown, Virginia

Opium . . . steam baths . . . marijuana . . . bloodletting . . . throw in a few leeches and you've got yourself one heckuva night on the town. But in colonial America, these were just a few of the treatments for what was—and still is today—a life-threatening disease: asthma. Like many of his fellow Virginia signers, Thomas Nelson enjoyed a life full of money, connections, and land. But no amount of cash or colonial-era medicine could ease his lifelong suffering from this disease, which eventually cost him his life.

He was born into a wealthy family in Yorktown, Virginia, and was schooled in England, as were most children of wealthy families at the time. He graduated from Cambridge, and when he returned to the colonies in 1761, he joined his father in managing the plantation and soon made his way into the mercantile business. He married Lucy Grymes a year after his return, and the couple eventually expanded their family to include at least eleven children. He had land, a good marriage, and the exceedingly fabulous social life that often went along with such wealth.

Considering his pedigree, Nelson was a shoo-in for Virginia's governing body, the House of Burgesses, where he sympathized with the plight of Bostonians and supported anti-British actions that protested the closing of Boston harbor. His patriotic views were surprising to some, considering the amount of time he had spent in England, but he later explained his beliefs in a letter to a friend, saying that he thought there was no "greater absurdity" than Americans having "affection for a people who are carrying on the most savage war against us."

In 1774, when Royal Governor Lord Dunmore learned that Virginia's Burgesses were allying themselves with Bostonians against the Crown, he disbanded the House. That hardly stopped Nelson and his fellow rabble-rousers. They simply collected their papers, quill pens, and walking sticks and moved to Williamsburg's Raleigh Tavern. Later that year, Nelson and a few compatriots further distinguished themselves by staging what is today referred to as the Yorktown Tea Party of 1774. On November 7, Nelson and other men from Yorktown boarded the British ship *Virginia*, which had carried tea from the motherland, and dumped its tea into the York River. The protestors later proudly boasted that they did no further damage to the ship, its crew, or any other cargo. (The Watermen's Museum in Yorktown hosts a reenactment of this event every November.)

Nelson was chosen as a delegate to the Continental Congress in 1775. In May 1776, the month Virginia delegates seized control of the royal government, Nelson made a motion to declare independence from Great Britain. His fellow Virginians approved the resolution. An enthusiastic Nelson carried the good news to Philadelphia, granting Richard Henry Lee permission to present his now-famous resolution for colony-wide independence on June 7, 1776.

Nelson wasn't the healthiest of men. In Congress, the ever-subtle John Adams described him as a "fat man," but then kindly added that he was "alert and lively for his weight," which must have been the polite, colonial-era equivalent for "big-boned" or "had a slow metabolism." In 1777, Nelson was forced to leave Congress after suffering from what has been described in older texts as a "disease of the head, probably of a paralytic nature." This may have been a mild stroke. And of course there was his asthma, an ailment that crippled its victims in this pre-inhaler era. Yet despite health problems, Nelson was made a brigadier general and placed in charge of the state's militia when invasion from the British seemed imminent.

Nelson was a dedicated leader, often using his own funds and supplies to support the war effort. In 1778, he responded to a general plea from Congress by assembling a troop of light cavalry and marching to Philadelphia to fight off the British. But upon arriving, they discovered they weren't needed—the British had already pulled back into New York. Nelson and his boys marched home, but things were far from over for General Nelson.

He was an excellent fund-raiser for the militia and often gave his own word and collateral, promising to make good on debts if the state could not. (But golly, the government would surely repay its debts, right?) He played an instrumental role in securing Virginia's portion of the funds needed to help the Continental Treasury pay the French fleet (and God knows the colonies needed the French at that point). Nelson raised a good chunk of the money himself and secured the loan with his own collateral, an act that would later come back to bite him in his big, fat bum.

In 1781, Nelson succeeded Thomas Jefferson as governor of Virginia while serving as a brigadier general in the state militia. Unlike many of his fellow signers who were militia members but never once packed a musket, Nelson had his military chops put to the test, most famously when he was commander of the Virginia militia at the siege of Yorktown. There is a popular story about his conduct during the siege of his hometown, namely that he ordered his own home to be fired upon because British general Cornwallis was headquartered there. The part about Cornwallis isn't entirely accurate. In reality, it appears Cornwallis was at a different home—that of the signer's uncle, "Secretary" Thomas Nelson—at the time.

Nelson didn't attack his uncle's home, but his own. During a strategy session, Nelson surmised that British officers were holed up at his residence, so he told the troops to have at them. It's also said that he offered the gunners five guineas for every hit. (There's no way to know if this is true.) Though his house was damaged in the battle, it wasn't completely demolished. You can still visit the restored Nelson House in Yorktown today. Be sure to look for the cannonballs lodged in the facade! Though evidence suggests that both the cannonballs and the holes themselves are from the Revolutionary War, the balls affixed to the facade are not likely the ones that did the damage. They were placed there after the fact, probably for appearance's sake.

Nelson's home wasn't his only asset damaged in the revolution. War wreaked havoc on his fortunes as well. His economic standing and mercantile business were headed downhill even before he started loaning money to the government, and when the notes came due on the loans he had secured for the nascent nation, he found ways to pay up, often selling land and slaves. In fact, in his will he instructed that parts of his land be sold to pay any leftover debts. Big shock—he was never repaid for the huge losses he incurred on behalf of the war. His heirs tried to recoup the money from the federal government, but they had no luck. Apparently Nelson was not the world's best bookkeeper.

Nelson's fortune may have been depleted, but he didn't exactly end his life in some Yorktown gutter, selling matches for ale money. He did move to a smaller estate later in life, where his poor health finally caught up with him just after his fiftieth birthday. He died at home of asthma in 1789 and was buried in Yorktown.

George Wythe

THE SIGNER WHO WAS POISONED BY HIS NEPHEW

BORN: About 1726

DIED: June 8, 1806

AGE AT SIGNING: About 50

PROFESSION: Lawyer, professor

BURIED: Saint John's Episcopal Churchyard, Richmond, Virginia

Despite vague suggestions to the contrary, no signer ever died at the hands of the British. In fact, only two signers died by violence. The first, Button Gwinnett, died in a duel only a year after signing the Declaration. The second was George Wythe, who was callously murdered when he was in his eighties.

With a prominent forehead and a few wisps of hair, Wythe (pronounced "with") seemed to be the physical embodiment of brainpower. Pennsylvania delegate Benjamin Rush called him "a profound lawyer," adding, "He seldom spoke in Congress, but when he did, his speeches were sensible, correct and pertinent. I have seldom known a man possess more modesty or a more dovelike simplicity and gentleness of manner." Thomas Jefferson was far more effusive in his praise. He called Wythe "my second father," "my faithful and beloved mentor in youth and my most affectionate friend through life," "my ancient master, my earliest and best friend."

Who was this man to receive such accolades? And why would anyone want to kill him?

The son of a planter, Wythe lost his father at the age of three. His unusually well-educated mother, Mary Walker Wythe, taught him at home as best she could before she, too, passed away. He studied law in an uncle's firm while in his teens and passed the bar at age twenty. His career was slow in taking off, but eventually he distinguished himself as an excellent attorney and an even better legal logician. Conscientious to a fault, he was said to drop clients known to lie. He had no desire to represent someone who wasn't scrupulously honest. A guy like that was probably best suited to the role of prosecutor, and for a while he worked well as an attorney general within the royal system. In 1754, he was elected to the House of Burgesses, Virginia's ruling body in the royal government of Virginia. He even served as mayor of Williamsburg.

Two things happened in the 1760s that impacted Wythe's life forever. The first: a young law student came to work at his firm, staying for a total of five years. That student: Thomas Jefferson. The two men bonded—both had lost fathers at a young age—and their warm friendship would last until Wythe's death. The second significant event of the decade was Parliament's passage of the Stamp Act in 1765, which sealed Wythe's fate as a patriot. The House of Burgesses asked him to draft a response on their behalf, and he crafted a document so scathing that the fearful Burgesses toned it down before accepting it.

In 1774, Wythe was sent to Congress, where he contributed significant legal concepts that shaped the American response to Britain. First, he suggested that America could become a separate but equal nation within the British Empire, much like the relationship that Canada and Australia have today with the United Kingdom. Wythe and signer Richard Henry Lee then insisted that Congress must hold the king, not Parliament, accountable for the colonists' miseries. If the king refused to right their wrongs, then they were legally entitled to make a break as an independent nation. Later, he was the first congressman to suggest forming alliances with other nations.

Despite his great influence, Wythe was not in Philadelphia during the July 2 vote, and he did not sign the declaration on August 2, 1776. For many years it was assumed he signed when he returned to Philadelphia in the fall, but some scholars now suggest—horrors!—that he may not have signed the Declaration of Independence at all, but rather authorized a clerk to act as his proxy. This theory developed because of a discrepancy between the way Wythe typically signed his name—"G. Wythe"—and its appearance on the Declaration—"George Wythe." It should be noted, however, that this hypothesis is unconfirmed, and Wythe is the only signer for whom this question has been raised.

Wythe left Congress in 1776 to help Thomas Jefferson set up Virginia's new government and legal code. He drafted the state constitution and designed the state seal. For a large part of his life, he taught law at the College of William and Mary, earning him recognition as the first law professor in the United States. He and his wife boarded young students and may have even paid for some of the poorer students' legal education. He loved the classics so much that he offered free classes to anyone who wanted to attend. In the late 1780s, he helped persuade Virginia's legislators to ratify the Constitution and is thus credited with helping Virginia become the tenth state.

Again, we have to ask: why would anyone want to kill such a kind, brilliant guy?

The answer has something to do with greed. Wythe had evolved into an ardent abolitionist, and when his second wife died, he freed his slaves. Unlike many former slave owners, he felt a certain obligation to them. Two of his former slaves lived with him and took care of him in his old age: Lydia Broadnax, his housekeeper, and Michael Brown, a young man whom Wythe liked and was tutoring. Both were to inherit part of Wythe's estate when he died.

Into this happy surrogate family came Wythe's own flesh and blood, George Wythe Sweeney, his sister's nineteen-year-old grandson. Sweeney was a troubled youth, a heavy drinker, and a gambler, but Wythe generously designated him to inherit the larger portion of the estate. Wythe's will also stated that if Broadnax and Brown died before Wythe, Sweeney would be entitled to his entire estate.

One morning, Broadnax observed Sweeney drinking his coffee from the kitchen coffee pot, then tossing a slip of white paper into the fire. Then Sweeney promptly left the house. Later that morning, the entire household drank from the same coffee pot, and all were seized with violent cramps. Broadnax recovered, but young

Brown died and Wythe became fatally ill. Aided by Broadnax, investigators pieced together what must have happened: Sweeney dumped arsenic in the pot, then burned the paper in which drugs and poisons were commonly wrapped in those days. Wythe lingered in painful agony for two weeks, but was lucid enough to instruct officials to search Sweeney's room for poison and to swear out a new will that disinherited Sweeney completely. Groaning, "I am murdered," Wythe died on June 8, 1806, at the presumed age of eighty. (His exact birth date is unknown.)

Sweeney was charged with the two murders and the forgery of some of his uncle's checks. Considering Wythe's lustrous career crafting Virginia's legal statutes, it's ironic that Broadnax's damning eyewitness testimony was inadmissible under the law because at that time blacks could not bear witness against white men. As a result, Sweeney was acquitted of the murders. He was convicted of forgery, but somehow he won a new trial that the prosecutors declined to pursue. Sweeney walked out of the courtroom a free man and vanished into history.

The murderer of George Wythe—the brilliant jurist who mentored presidents Thomas Jefferson and James Monroe, Chief Justice John Marshall, and House Speaker and Secretary of State Henry Clay—was set free on a legal technicality.

George Wythe

XI.

North Carolina

Joseph Hewes

THE SIGNER WHO WORKED HIMSELF TO DEATH

BORN: January 23, 1730

DIED: October 10, 1779

AGE AT SIGNING: 46

PROFESSION: Merchant, shipping magnate

BURIED: Somewhere in Christ Church Burial Ground, Philadelphia, Pennsylvania

A Quaker who supported revolution, a bachelor who died with a broken heart, Joseph Hewes buried himself in his work and drove himself to an early grave. But before he checked out, he played a pivotal role in securing the vote for independence.

None of the North Carolina signers were born in their adopted state. Quaker-born Joseph Hewes grew up on an estate outside Princeton, New Jersey, and eventually attended college at the future Ivy League institution. After graduation, he apprenticed to a merchant in Philadelphia and later started his own mercantile business. Around 1760, he moved down to Edenton, North Carolina, a growing seaport on the Albemarle Sound, and worked in the shipping and import/export business with his nephew Nathaniel Allen Jr. Before long he had a tidy little pile of money all his own. Unfortunately, he didn't have the same good luck in his personal life. The love of his life, Isabella Johnston, died just days before their wedding. *Cue violins* . . .

On the bright side, being a wealthy, single, and personable man went as far in the 1700s as it does today, so Hewes was both popular and respected. In 1766, he became involved with the provincial assembly and was an advocate for the rights and freedom of the colonies, even though he did not initially think that separating from Britain was the best means to achieving that end.

He was elected to the First Continental Congress in 1774 and sat on the committee that drew up a declaration of rights of the colonies and helped develop Congress's plan for nonimportation, which boycotted the importation of British goods. Considering Hewes was an importer by trade, the nonimportation pill would have been a tough one to swallow. But he gulped it down anyway, despite the impact it would likely have on his livelihood.

In 1775, the pacifist Quakers spoke out against the Continental Congress and their activities, opposing the idea of any violent revolution. Hewes broke with his Quaker faith, and only he really knows if it was for his love of independence, his love of dancing, or maybe a little of both. He was, after all, still a bachelor, and a high-steppin' Virginia reel was a great way to make time with the ladies. But although he may have been enchanted by them, he—like signer Caesar Rodney—remained a bachelor to the end of his days.

When Richard Henry Lee made his resolution to split with

Britain in June 1776, Hewes still felt the action was premature. He initially opposed the resolution, despite the fact that North Carolina's legislature was among the first to give its delegates the go-ahead to vote in favor of independence. But a rousing speech by John Adams finally won Hewes over. Adams wrote about Hewes and his role in turning the tide toward independence on several occasions: "Mr. Hewes, who had hitherto constantly voted against it, started upright, and lifting up both hands to Heaven . . . cried out, 'It is done! and I will abide by it.'" Adams later said, "The unanimity of the States finally depended upon the vote of Joseph Hewes, and was finally determined by him."

While in Congress, Hewes's shipping background came in quite handy. He played a leading role on the marine committee and helped establish the Continental navy. Today he is commonly referred to as the first secretary of the navy. Perhaps his biggest naval accomplishment was appointing his friend John Paul Jones as an officer and getting him a ship. Jones, of course, went on to become the most celebrated naval hero of the Revolutionary War.

Hewes served in the North Carolina legislature in 1777 and returned to Congress in 1779. By then he was already ill, most likely from a combination of overwork and undernourishment. Without a wife and family to head home to at night, he thought nothing of working twelve-hour days, foregoing food, drink, and downtime. "My country is entitled to my services, and I shall not shrink from her cause, even though it should cost me my life," he reportedly said. These words came back to haunt him that fall when, at just forty-nine years old and too sick to travel home, Hewes died and was buried in Philadelphia. His funeral was attended by Congress, the general assembly of Pennsylvania, and many other dignitaries. Congressmen wore a crape around their arms for a month as a sign of mourning.

Joseph Hewes,

William Hooper

THE SIGNER WHO FEARED DEMOCRACY

BORN: June 17, 1742

DIED: October 14, 1790

AGE AT SIGNING: 34

PROFESSION: Lawyer

BURIED: Guilford Courthouse National Military Park, Greensboro, North Carolina

It took a lot to impress John Adams, and William Hooper had all the right stuff. Adams regarded him as one of the finest speakers in Congress and likened him to two famous orators: Richard Henry Lee, the Virginia signer who introduced the resolution calling for independence, and Patrick Henry, the renowned Virginia radical who has been forever linked with the famous "Give me Liberty, or give me death" speech (even though he probably never uttered those words).

A minister's son, Hooper was born in Boston and graduated from Harvard while still in his teens. Early in his career as a lawyer, he made the unusual decision to move from New England to the South. Most historians assume he was looking for an untapped market for his practice, though others insist that the burgeoning rebel didn't want to embarrass his family, which was loyal to the Crown. This latter theory is hard to believe, because Hooper was sympathetic to Loyalists. Besides, if he wanted to avoid embarrassing a family loyal to the Crown, he sure went about it the wrong way. After becoming a leading attorney in Wilmington, along North Carolina's coast, he married a woman named Anne Clark, the daughter of local Loyalists (whom he promptly embarrassed).

It's hard to shake one's upbringing. Hooper may have been a radical, a rebel, and a patriot, but he would forever be an aristocrat. As a young attorney general, he became enmeshed in a political uprising, begun in the 1760s, known as the Regulator Movement, or the War of Regulation. Simply put, poor North Carolinian settlers had become fed up with what they perceived as corruption, excessive fees, and taxation by the ruling elite and their enforcers, usually sheriffs. Hooper, in his role as attorney, was seen by the mob as part of the larger problem, and he was attacked by vigilante Regulators. Some sources say he was beaten or harassed in a courtroom, while others say he was dragged through the streets. The experience left an indelible impression: the unwashed masses were not to be trusted. Perhaps because of this experience, Hooper was leery of mob rule, and of democracy in general, for the rest of his life.

Beginning about 1773, Hooper wrote letters supporting the American cause and served on North Carolina's first Provincial Congress, where he was highly regarded as a gifted spokesman for American rights. In an April 1774 letter to his friend James Iredell,

Hooper wrote: "[The colonies] are striding fast to independence, and will, ere long, build an empire upon the ruins of Great Britain—will adopt its constitution, purged of its impurities; and from an experience of its defects, will guard against those evils which have wasted its vigor and brought it to an untimely end." This letter—thought to be the first prediction of American independence—is the reason Hooper is dubbed the "prophet of independence." (He's also known as "the misunderstood patriot." We'll see why shortly.)

Hooper was elected to the Continental Congress in 1774 and served until 1777. Although he supported the Lee Resolution, Hooper was away on business during the critical vote. He returned to Philadelphia in time to sign the famous document in August. He was the youngest North Carolina signer, only thirty-four years old. Upon leaving Congress he returned home, determined to shore up his failing fortune. In those days, serving in Congress brought with it serious financial consequences. Paying room and board in Philadelphia, all while shelling out cash for a family you never saw back home, was enough to impoverish most men.

Hooper appears to have suffered greatly during the war, though the specifics of his loss are murky. In January 1781, the British arrived at the Cape Fear River, which runs through the heart of Wilmington. Hooper likely possessed two homes in the area, one in town and another closer to the beach. Both were destroyed. Hooper and his family separated, and he fled to the North Carolina backcountry, relying on friends for shelter and food. While on the run, he contracted malaria, which plagued him with fever, chills, and flulike symptoms until the end of his days. Hooper and his family were reunited after the British left the area, but in 1782 they relocated to a home in Hillsborough, just northwest of Durham.

Hooper lived for only another eight years. He served in the new state legislature, but was never a popular leader. Lacking the common touch, he was an aloof politician who continued to fear democracy and the possibility that it might descend into mob rule. Loyalists hated him for his anti-British beliefs; patriots hated him for blocking reprisals against Loyalists. Hooper also found himself arguing against his colleagues about the new U.S. Constitution and his belief in a strong federal government, a sentiment many of his fellow North Carolinians strongly opposed. Though he had signed the greatest document in the land, he was a distrusted and misunderstood patriot for the rest of his days.

He lived just long enough to see the Constitution ratified. Sapped by illness, Hooper died in Hillsborough at age forty-eight. He was buried on his property, but his remains—and those of signer John Penn—were moved more than one hundred years later to the Guilford Courthouse Military Park in Greensboro, North Carolina. Theirs is a fine monument in a lovely, parklike setting, though neither had anything to do with the battle fought there against the British in 1781.

John Penn

THE SIGNER WHO TAUGHT HIMSELF HOW TO READ AND WRITE

BORN: May 6, 1740

DIED: September 14, 1788

AGE AT SIGNING: 36

PROFESSION: Lawyer

BURIED: Guilford Courthouse Military Park, Greensboro, North Carolina

John Penn's biographies, like his political career, are short. He had one shining moment of glory in Philadelphia, then retired to be a country lawyer in an obscure North Carolina town, where he died at the age of forty-eight. Apart from signing the Declaration, he is remembered for having adroitly reasoned his way out of shooting a man in a duel.

Penn was born outside Fredericksburg, Virginia, to a farmer and the daughter of a country judge. The family appears to have been well-off, but Penn's father didn't think much of book-learning, so he provided his son with only two or three years of education. Realizing he could barely scribble his own name, eighteen-year-old Penn befriended a lawyer cousin, seeking help. Penn was seriously deficient compared to most wealthy men his age. (Nearly all the highborn signers had graduated from college by his age.) Penn had a lot of catching up to do. In the span of only three years, he borrowed books from his cousin's library, taught himself to read and write, began working in the man's law practice, and was ultimately admitted to the bar by age twenty-one. He married Susannah Lyme and practiced law in Virginia for about a decade before they moved over the North Carolina border to Granville County, northeast of Durham.

A quick study, Penn always seemed to impress people and thus landed greater responsibilities. He'd only been living in North Carolina two years when he signed the Declaration of Independence on behalf of his new home. Penn doesn't appear to have had doubts about independence, as did his fellow North Carolinians William Hooper and Joseph Hewes. On February 12, 1776, while in Philadelphia, Penn wrote a letter to Thomas Person, brigadier general in the North Carolina militia. In his words, we hear obvious passion: "For God's sake my Good Sir, encourage our People, animate them to dare even to die for their country. Our struggle I hope will not continue long—may unanimity and success crown your endeavours."

In April, North Carolina held a critical meeting in Halifax, at which the colony's leading men became convinced that a break with Britain was not only imminent, but necessary. In a document called the Halifax Resolves, this body instructed Penn, Hooper, and Hewes to vote for independence. When the big day came, Hooper was out of town, but Hewes and Penn cast their votes in favor of independence. All three signed the Declaration on August 2.

During his days in Philadelphia, Penn was perceived as a "good-humored man" who was chatty among friends but didn't say much in Congress. This was odd, since he was known to be a forceful orator in the courtroom, and some historians claim he was capable of reducing the court and jury to tears.

The only time we have evidence of him losing his cool was when he squabbled with a South Carolinian named Henry Laurens, John Hancock's successor as president of Congress. The reason for their disagreement is lost, but Laurens challenged Penn to a duel. These standoffs, which date back to the Middle Ages, were a commonly accepted way to settle disputes between two parties. The belief was that duels limited the collateral damage and prevented the likelihood of all-out feuds between noble families. Each culture has its own etiquette—or *code duello*—for staging duels. Penn and Laurens would have named the time and place of the duel, chosen weapons, selected witnesses, and even arranged for the presence of a medic. According to the code, the time-honored way of getting out of a duel was to "throw away your fire"—very obviously shooting one's weapon at the ground. This was the signal that you still had the chutzpah to show up at the duel, but you weren't in the mood to kill or be killed today. Your opponent then did the same, and you both saved face.

Penn found a remarkably sane way to get out of the duel without firing a single shot. Since he and Laurens lived at the same Philadelphia boarding house, the two met for breakfast on the appointed date. After dining together, they headed to the duel site on Chestnut Street. As they were crossing Fifth Street, they came across a deep puddle in the dirt. Penn turned to help the older, heavier man across the gully.

In that moment, something must have clicked in Penn's lawyerly brain. He probably thought: "This is ludicrous! How can I take steak and eggs with a guy, help him across the street, then blow his brains out?" Penn immediately offered to drop the whole thing, and Laurens agreed.

Penn served in Congress until 1780, becoming the senior delegate from his state. He was one of sixteen Declaration signers who also signed the Articles of Confederation. Then he worked on the war board of his new state and helped organize the region's defense as General Charles Cornwallis and his troops marched north from South Carolina into Virginia. Penn's health troubled him, forcing him to retire from politics in 1781.

None of the North Carolina signers lived beyond age fifty. Penn was dead at forty-eight. Survived by his wife and three children, he was buried on the grounds of his home. Later he was reinterred under a signer's monument, along with William Hooper, at the Guilford Courthouse Military Park in Greensboro.

John Penn

XII.
South Carolina

Thomas Lynch Jr.

THE SIGNER BURIED AT THE BOTTOM OF THE SEA

BORN: August 5, 1749

DIED: About 1779

AGE AT SIGNING: 26

PROFESSION: Lawyer, planter

BURIED: Atlantic Ocean

Thomas Lynch Jr. was never meant to sign the Declaration of Independence. But what began as filial duty evolved into an opportunity to participate in the creation of the most famous document in American history.

Young Lynch was a rich planter's son who had enjoyed every advantage. He had a beautiful young wife and a plantation that his father had given to him on the South Santee River, northeast of Charleston. At age twenty-six, he was the second youngest of the four men South Carolina sent to Philadelphia. All four—Lynch Jr., Arthur Middleton, Thomas Heyward Jr., and Edward Rutledge—had studied law at a hallowed law guild in London. All were under the age of thirty-four, and all were perceived as over-privileged dandies.

Why did South Carolina send such young men to Congress? The simple answer is that they didn't have anyone else. South Carolina wanted strong local government. The colony wanted to govern itself, period, and had mixed feelings regarding the matter of national independence. Was being governed by a bunch of northern ideologues any better than being ruled by the British? In 1774, they sent Thomas Lynch Sr. to Philadelphia. He was a South Carolina delegate descended from Irishmen who had prospered in America. His people had long hated the Crown, and Lynch Sr.— a radical despite his vast wealth and lands—could be relied upon not to rashly empower a new government. But early in 1776, the elderly Lynch suffered a stroke and was unable to leave his bed. Casting about for a substitute, South Carolina decided to send his son Thomas Jr. to tend to his father's care and vote in Congress on various matters in his father's stead. They tossed in three other delegates, all equally young, because they couldn't spare anyone with more experience. Having ousted the royal government, South Carolina was busy crafting a new constitution and setting up a provisional legislative body.

Cut loose from his other political chores, the dutiful son scampered to Philly to tend to his father. The Lynches were the only father-son team serving in Congress at the same time, but it seems clear that Thomas Sr. did not do much in Congress following his stroke. Though Thomas Jr. had been exposed to malaria during military service in South Carolina and was himself sick, he still managed to monitor the debates in Congress throughout that long, hot, humid summer. At night, he hurried back to their Philadelphia flat and briefed his ailing father on the events of the day. Ultimately, Thomas Jr. and his fellow delegates—the rich, entitled men who might have seemed unlikely to vote for independence—voted for and signed the Declaration.

The elder Lynch was too sick to attend either event. In fact, if you look on the Declaration, you'll see that a space was left between Rutledge's and Heyward's signatures for the elder Lynch to sign. He never did. In fact, he died in Annapolis on the way home to South Carolina. His son, the replacement signer, was with him at the end, and as his father's only son, he inherited his family's vast estate. You'd think the guy had it all: wealth, looks, a pretty wife, productive lands, and numerous slaves to work them. But Thomas Jr. was still ill, and doctors suggested that he nurse himself back to health in a sunny locale.

In 1779, at the age of thirty, sickly Thomas embarked on a trip to the south of France by way of the West Indies. He and Elizabeth boarded a ship in South Carolina and sailed down the east coast of America toward the Caribbean. It's believed that they got as far as modern-day Statia, in the Netherlands Antilles. Their next ship, to Europe, most likely hit a storm, because the two were never seen again. Thomas Lynch Jr., the second-youngest signer, was also the youngest of all fifty-six men to be wiped off the face of the earth.

Recently the sad lives of the Lynches made modern-day news. In 2008, a gold mourning ring believed to have belonged to Thomas Sr. surfaced at an antiques show in Charleston. Mourning jewelry was crafted at the behest of wealthy families to commemorate the death of loved ones. An inscription indicates that Thomas Sr. wore the ring to remember his wife, Elizabeth, the mother of the signer. An Annapolis family had carefully preserved the precious object for two hundred years, though no one knows how it came to be in their possession. Did Thomas Jr. offer the ring in lieu of payment for medical services for his ailing father, who died in Annapolis? Or was the ring pilfered from the grieving son as he returned home after signing the Declaration, as some believe? This mystery is lost to time, but fortunately the ring is not. Within two hours of the show's opening it was purchased, for an undisclosed five-figure sum, by an anonymous buyer, who vowed that the ring will never again leave the state of South Carolina. Though fate conspired to keep the Lynches from dying on their native soil, perhaps father and son would have taken comfort in knowing that this family heirloom has finally returned home.

Arthur Middleton

THE SIGNER ALSO KNOWN AS ANDREW MARVELL

BORN: June 26, 1742

DIED: January 1, 1787

AGE AT SIGNING: 34

PROFESSION: Planter, lawyer

BURIED: Middleton Place, Charleston, South Carolina

Of the four young signers from South Carolina who put their name on the Declaration of Independence, thirty-four-year-old Arthur Middleton was the oldest. He was also probably the richest. But all his money did little good when he was imprisoned by British soldiers for more than a year.

Born at Middleton Place on the Ashley River, near Charleston, Arthur Middleton came from a family possessing about 50,000 acres and 800 slaves. His father, Henry Middleton, stood with the patriots early on and was president of the First Continental Congress. The younger Middleton was extremely patriotic; it's rumored that he supported the tarring and feathering of anyone with ties to the Crown. For someone with such strong views (not to mention a pretty fierce temper), it's a little surprising that he sometimes wrote under the pen name "Andrew Marvell."

"Mr. Marvell" served on various committees and helped arrange for his colony's soon-to-be-needed defenses. He was also instrumental in very wisely arranging to get hold of the public store of arms before any of the royal appointees, including the governor, could do the same.

At the beginning of 1776, Middleton Jr. was working on a committee to form a new government for South Carolina and to draw up the state's new Constitution. It was adopted in March, making South Carolina the second colony—after New Hampshire—to announce a government separate from King George's.

When Middleton Sr. decided not to return to the Continental Congress, Arthur took his place. He made an impression—all the South Carolinians did, for their fashion sense if nothing else—and his temper was well documented. Fellow signer Benjamin Rush described him to be "a man of cynical temper, but of upright intentions toward his country. . . . He spoke frequently, and always with asperity or personalities." Middleton notably refused to serve on the committee of accounts because he said he didn't understand them and didn't like business.

This attitude probably didn't do much to improve the image of the South Carolina delegates as spoiled rich plantation kids. John Adams, who had lots to say about the fancy foursome, offered this little nugget about Middleton: "He had little information and less argument; in rudeness and sarcasm his forte lay, and he played off his artillery without reserve."

South Carolina and Pennsylvania were the only two colonies to vote against independence on July 1. (New York abstained and Delaware was deadlocked.) But the following day South Carolina voted "yes" for the sake of unanimity, and Middleton signed in August, along with most of the other delegates.

In the final years of the war, the southern colonies took center stage. In May 1780, Middleton was serving in the militia and was captured during the siege of Charleston. Along with cosigners Edward Rutledge and Thomas Heyward Jr., he was imprisoned in St. Augustine, Florida, reportedly in the Castillo de San Marcos—called Fort St. Marks by the British. However, recent evidence suggests that he and the others were held under house arrest and would have avoided the dismal conditions at Fort St. Marks. Officers were sometimes treated better than enlisted soldiers, if only to ensure that British officers would receive similar treatment. This tit-for-tat attitude ultimately helped free the South Carolinians. In July 1781, they were released as part of a prisoner exchange.

After the war, there were a lot of folks who thought that Tories and those who had done business with the Brits should have their property confiscated. Middleton, along with Rutledge, stood against this, despite their fourteen months in captivity. Middleton had come a long way from his support of tarring and feathering.

When he returned home, Middleton found the structures on his property had been left mostly intact, but his paintings had been trashed and slashed, some two hundred of his slaves were sold off, and the silver was long gone. During the war, his wife, Mary, had had to beg the British commissioner for the return of some of her property so that she could take care of her family, and the British complied (possibly thanks to some Loyalist relatives on her side of the family).

Middleton was again appointed to Congress and served until 1782, when he returned home to his life as a planter and worked to rebuild Middleton Place and the rest of his lands. He served on and off in the state legislature until 1787 and was also one of the original trustees of the College of Charleston. Though his work on the third committee assigned to create the Great Seal of the United States didn't make the cut—the design that finally got the thumbs-up was put together by secretary of Congress Charles Thomson—Middleton is credited with having designed the reverse of the seal of South Carolina, which is now incorporated into the current one-sided design. His contribution features the Roman goddess Spes, or "Hope," and the motto "While I breathe, I hope." At just forty-four years old, Middleton stopped breathing—and hoping—on New Year's Day, 1787, leaving a wife and nine children behind.

Edward Rutledge

THE SIGNER WHO DELAYED INDEPENDENCE BY A MONTH

BORN: November 23, 1749

DIED: January 23, 1800

AGE AT SIGNING: 26

PROFESSION: Lawyer, planter

BURIED: Saint Philip's Church Cemetery, Charleston, South Carolina

According to Merriam-Webster, a dandy is "a man who gives exaggerated attention to personal appearance." Edward Rutledge is often portrayed as the dandy of the Continental Congress, a young southern gentleman of privilege who probably cared a little too much for the clothes and finery, especially when compared to some of the more Puritan men among the Founding Fathers.

Rutledge had first attended the Continental Congress in 1774, joining his father-in-law Henry Middleton and his political powerhouse brother John. But by spring 1776, retirements, illness, and a preoccupation on the part of South Carolina with its new

colonial government left Rutledge in charge of the state's delegation to Philadelphia, where he was joined by his brother-in-law
Arthur Middleton, Thomas Lynch Jr., and Thomas Heyward Jr.
All four were cut from the same imported silk cloth: they were all
loaded, all products of the plantation aristocracy, and all trained
in law. The South Carolina delegation boasted an average age
between twenty-nine and thirty. Yet despite their youth, the
group, especially Rutledge, made quite an impact in Congress.

Rutledge was an active and effectual speaker in Congress and
one of the leading voices responsible for postponing until July the
vote on Lee's June 7 resolution for independence. In a sense, Americans have him to thank for their ability to celebrate independence
during a time of year that's perfect for baseball, hot dogs, apple
pies, and ice cream.

Combine Rutledge's tendency to debate with his frilly sleeves
and initial reluctance to vote for independence, and it's no wonder
John Adams had such nasty things to say about him. When the
young guns of South Carolina showed up in Congress, Adams
noted that they were "a young, smart, spirited body." But after just
a few bouts of verbal sparring, Adams was describing Rutledge as
"a perfect Bob-o-Lincoln—a swallow, a sparrow, a peacock; excessively vain, excessively weak, and excessively variable and unsteady;
jejeune, inane and puerile." Jejeune? Ouch. But when Adams
referred to Rutledge as "uncouth and ungraceful," well, that must
have been the end of invitations to the Rutledge plantation for old
Mr. Adams.

It's not that Rutledge was unpatriotic. He simply thought—
much like the Pennsylvanians—that declaring independence was

a bit premature. Why not develop a proper army and get some allies first? When the preliminary vote was taken on July 1, 1776, South Carolina voted against independence. But Rutledge saw which way the wind was blowing—nine of the colonies had voted in favor of declaring independence—and he valued unanimity. So on July 2, he and his cohorts put on some very pretty clothes and showed up to vote in favor of declaring a break from Great Britain.

Even though Rutledge agreed to independence, he still had plenty to say during the debates over the language of the Declaration. Jefferson's original draft contained language decrying the "execrable commerce" of slavery and the Crown's role in it. Rutledge was one of the more vocal delegates of South Carolina and Georgia, the two states that still allowed the importation of slaves. He is often credited with playing a pivotal role in getting the anti-slavery language removed. So the slavery debate was left, in part at least, for another day and another war, one in which South Carolina would again assume great importance.

Once the document was agreed upon, Rutledge signed, and he is generally described as the youngest person to do so (but you can read a conflicting account on page 269).

During the Revolutionary War, Rutledge served as a captain in the Charleston Battalion of Artillery, and helped to defend Charleston in 1779 as the British loomed large off-shore. During the siege of Charleston, Rutledge and two of his fellow signers from South Carolina, Arthur Middleton and Thomas Heyward Jr., were taken prisoner. They were held in St. Augustine from May 1780 until July 1781, when they were released in a prisoner exchange. Rutledge's mother was also arrested, removed from her home, and forced to live under house arrest in Charleston, where the British or Loyalists could keep a better eye on her. The British suspected that the spunky old dame had information they might find useful.

After the war, Rutledge was able to recover his property and finances. He continued to serve South Carolina, first as a member of the state legislature and later as governor, though he died before completing a full term. He suffered from gout, the most popular disease in Congress, and his demise at age fifty was said to have been hurried along by either exposure to cold and rain in Columbia or the death of George Washington in December 1799, an event that was said to have upset him gravely.

Thomas Heyward Jr.

THE SIGNER-SONGWRITER

BORN: July 28, 1746

DIED: March 6, 1809

AGE AT SIGNING: 30

PROFESSION: Lawyer, planter

BURIED: Heyward family plot, outside Ridgeland, South Carolina

Thomas Heyward Jr. is one of two signers (along with Francis Hopkinson of New Jersey) who wrote a song available for download from iTunes—maybe. The issue isn't whether mp3s of eighteenth-century ditties are available online. They are, in droves. The real question is whether Thomas Heyward Jr.—a man once described as possessing "elegant poetical genius"—really wrote the song ascribed to him. No one knows for sure, but the story tugs at the heartstrings.

Like all the young men who signed for South Carolina, Heyward was the son of a rich planter. He studied law in London and returned home to begin practicing at the age of twenty-five. Soon after, he married and settled into White Hall, a massive plantation home not far from his father's place.

His parish sent him to the colonial legislature, which was squabbling with the governor over—what else?—taxes. While in London, Heyward had formed a disagreeable impression of the motherland. Brits, he was rankled to find, looked down upon those born in the colonies. South Carolinians were typically proud of their heritage, so much that they often held themselves apart from the other colonies.

However, this did not mean that Heyward and his fellow colonists could ignore the plight of the Bostonians. When Parliament closed the port of Boston in response to the Boston Tea Party, South Carolina feared its ports were vulnerable to similar actions and in turn called a convention to formulate a plan. What they did was simple: they ousted the royal governor, set up a new government, and wrote a new constitution—rationalizing it all by saying that such measures would remain in place only until differences with the mother country were resolved.

Heyward worked on the committee that was drafting the new constitution, but his fellow citizens needed a voice in Congress. Heyward, then about thirty, was sent to Philadelphia with three other young dandies, Edward Rutledge, Arthur Middleton, and Thomas Lynch Jr. Heyward was the second-oldest in the group. He arrived in Congress and stood out as being "a firm republican of good education and most amiable manners."

Though the young men had not been instructed to vote for independence, they quickly grasped that if the thirteen colonies did not present a unified front, the union of states could not function. On July 2, they reversed their stance and sided with the other colonies. Heyward, like the others, voted for and signed the Declaration. (In 1778, his last year in Congress, he signed the Articles of Confederation as well.)

The war brought adversity to Heyward's life. He served as a captain in the militia, and in 1779, he was wounded in an attack on Port Royal Island, north of Hilton Head on the South Carolina coast. The next year, the British ransacked White Hall plantation, leading away his slaves, many of whom were sold to Jamaican sugar plantations. Heyward would recover some of them, but about 130 were lost for good. Heyward himself was captured in May 1780, when the British attacked Charleston. At first, he was paroled, but the authorities later changed their minds. He was rearrested and imprisoned, first on a prison ship, then in St. Augustine, Florida. His fellow prisoners included Rutledge and Middleton.

While imprisoned, Heyward occupied his mind by writing songs. Imagine, then, that the sun begins to rise off the coast of Florida on the morning of July 4, 1781. Unshaven and dressed in rags, Heyward and his fellow signers stand to face the new day on the fifth anniversary of the adoption of the Declaration of Independence. As the British guards try to silence them, they stand on crude bunks and belt out a tune Heyward has crafted in prison. The melody is taken from "God Save the King," the British national anthem. But the words have been changed to something far more American. One version of the song, entitled "God Save the Thirteen States," begins:

God save the Thirteen States!
Long rule the United States!

God save our States!
Make us victorious,
Happy and glorious;
No tyrants over us;
God save our States!

Imagine what a poignant, *Les Miz* moment that would have been! Unfortunately, recent evidence suggests that their conditions under house arrest were fairly decent. No rags to be found. And in fact this folk song (which was popular in the United States during this period) has been attributed to a number of other authors—so until someone unearths a scrap of lyrics in Heyward's handwriting, signed and notarized, its true authorship may never be known.

His incarceration lasted until July 1781, when he (along with Rutledge and Middleton) was released as part of a prisoner exchange. Though he served as a judge and state legislator later in life, Heyward mostly retired from politics and devoted himself to rebuilding White Hall plantation and growing his crops. He lived longer than any other South Carolina signer, dying in 1809 at age sixty-three. He was buried at his father's estate, Old House. The plantation was destroyed during the Civil War and lies in marshy ruins today, but the grave of the signer, surrounded by a low wall of lichen-covered bricks, is still accessible down a lonely drive lined with oak trees.

Perhaps it's fitting that the signer-songwriter's many descendants include Dubose Heyward, the author of the novel that became the basis for the opera *Porgy and Bess.*

XIII.

Georgia

Lyman Hall

THE SIGNER WHO DRAGGED GEORGIA INTO THE UNION

BORN: April 12, 1724

DIED: October 19, 1790

AGE AT SIGNING: 52

PROFESSION: Physician, minister, planter

BURIED: First in Burke County, Georgia, and then moved to Courthouse Grounds, Augusta, Georgia

Though Lyman Hall dabbled in a number of vocations, he was as focused as they came with regard to fighting for America's freedom. And as that fight wore on, he helped lead the most fence-straddling of the colonies to sign on for separation from Britain. Of course, this was after he took matters into his own hands and carried them all the way to Philadelphia—without Georgia's blessing.

Born and raised in Connecticut, Hall attended Yale with the intention of becoming a minister. But when he began preaching in 1749, things did not go as planned. Hall knocked heads with the congregation and was dismissed. After some time filling in at local churches when a pulpit was empty, he changed his career to medicine and apprenticed with a physician. Soon Hall also started a family, and though his first wife, Abigail Burr, died roughly a year after they were wed, he remarried a couple of years later to Mary Osborn and they had a son.

The Hall family decided to move south. They landed first in Dorchester, South Carolina, and soon joined a group of transplanted New Englanders and headed even farther south, to St. John's Parish in the Midway District along the Georgia coast. There, about 1758, the group founded Sunbury, which became a seaport hub. They set to work planting crops, including rice and indigo. The swampy, malarial messes that needed to be drained for the rice planting produced enough disease-carrying mosquitoes to keep good doctor Hall busy. He soon set up his own plantation, Hall's Knoll, nearby.

Sunbury then was probably a lot like Boca Raton today—everyone was a Yankee transplant. Because of its ties to family and friends in the north, Sunbury became a center for the patriot cause in an otherwise Loyalist area, which led St. John's Parish to eventually be called the "southern cradle of liberty."

Georgia was the most remote of the colonies and very sparsely populated. For these reasons, it enjoyed a nonthreatening relationship with the Crown, and therefore Sunbury's patriotic sentiments were not representative of the majority opinion in the colony by any means. In summer 1774, Hall traveled to Savannah to discuss the potential of a colonial revolution and left frustrated with the results and inaction, especially since Georgia was not planning to—and did not—send any delegates to the First Continental Congress later that year.

At the provincial convention in Savannah the following January, nothing much had changed. Georgia opted not to adopt the congressional proposal for a Continental Association, a voluntary embargo on trade with Great Britain until the pesky disagreements between the colonies and the Crown were settled.

Hall disagreed with Georgia's continued lack of gumption. Under his leadership, St. John's contacted South Carolina, proposing that the parish join South Carolina in its boycott on British goods and other patriot-minded agreements. St. John's didn't want to secede from Georgia; it just wanted its voice heard, and the only way to get a vote was to unite with a colony with a presence in Congress. South Carolina refused the offer, citing legislative reasons, and perhaps the fact that Sunbury was forty-plus miles from the South Carolina border. So St. John's remained a patriotic parish in a Loyalist colony.

In March 1775, St. John's, tired of not getting along with the other kids, decided to pick up their ball and go home. They withdrew from Georgia's legislative body, held their own convention, and voted to send a delegate of their choosing to the Continental Congress, with or without Georgia's consent. When Hall arrived in Philadelphia in May as the representative of a single Georgia county, the congressional boys in Philly weren't sure what to do with him. But they liked his spunk and knew they would need a voice in Georgia for the revolution to succeed. They admitted Hall as a nonvoting member. In July 1775—likely inspired to action by the battles at Lexington, Concord, Fort Ticonderoga, and Bunker Hill—Georgia got on board, acknowledged Hall's presence at Congress, and sent four other delegates to join him.

In February 1776, Hall returned to Congress with George Walton and his friend Button Gwinnett. No instructions were given to Georgia delegates beyond the general counsel that they could exercise their own opinions and do what they thought was best for the common good. Walton and Hall immediately aligned with John Adams, associating themselves with the other "violents" in Congress. Georgia happily voted for independence, and the three signers penned their names to the document.

In 1778, the British were hitting the south hard, and Hall's plantation was destroyed. He moved his family north—probably back to Connecticut—to ride out the rest of the war. When the coast was clear (literally!), he relocated to Savannah and hung out his doctor's shingle once more, hoping to repair his wrecked finances.

But Hall wasn't done with public service just yet. He served as Georgia's governor from 1783 to 1784 and worked to get the state's economy on track, made treaties with the Cherokee, and recommended a land grant be set aside for a college, the beginnings of Franklin College and the University of Georgia, America's first state-chartered university. Hall sold the land at Hall's Knoll and in 1790 moved to Burke County, where he purchased the Shell Bluff Plantation. He didn't get to enjoy his new home for long though; he died later the same year. He was buried on the plantation until—as often seems to happen with the signers—his remains were moved. He now rests beneath a monument honoring the signers in Augusta.

Lyman Hall

George Walton

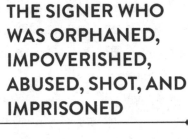

THE SIGNER WHO WAS ORPHANED, IMPOVERISHED, ABUSED, SHOT, AND IMPRISONED

BORN: Between 1741 and 1753

DIED: February 2, 1804

AGE AT SIGNING: About 35

PROFESSION: Lawyer

BURIED: First at Rosney Cemetery, then moved to Courthouse Grounds, Augusta, Georgia

Though many of the signers held positions in their state militia, the number who actually saw battle, let alone were wounded or captured, is considerably smaller. But George Walton, a poor, orphaned child and self-made success story, survived a gunshot wound and imprisonment at the hands of the British before stepping into the roles of governor and senator from Georgia.

Born in Virginia and orphaned very young, Walton was poor. He was taken in by an uncle who apprenticed him to a local carpenter. There are two competing stories of the carpenter's treatment of young George. One paints him as a mean man who was so opposed to Walton's desire to educate himself that he refused to give the boy a proper candle so he could read his books. In this version of the story, the indomitable young Walton gathered wood chips so he could set them ablaze and, by the meager glow, read whatever books he could get his little calloused hands on. The opposing story portrays the carpenter as a kindly old man who actually let Walton take time off work to attend school. It's hard to determine which account of Walton's apprenticeship is true, but there is no doubt that Walton was poor and uneducated and had a rough time of it, especially when compared to the more pampered and wealthy signers. Yet still he managed, despite little formal schooling, to educate himself well enough that he was able to study with a lawyer when he moved to Savannah, Georgia, in his twenties.

An active patriot, Walton was largely responsible for shaping Savannah into Georgia's "other" Whig outpost (the first being signer Lyman Hall's St. John's Parish) in a predominantly Loyalist and noncommittal colony. In summer 1774, he helped organize a series of meetings at Tondee's Tavern to discuss Georgia's role in the developing revolution. The gatherings sparked much debate but little action. Walton hoped that others in the province would be inspired to follow St. John's lead in the march toward independence, but he didn't have much luck in convincing them to do so. The majority of the remote and sparsely populated colony chose to maintain the status quo to such an extent that Georgia did not send any representatives to the First Continental Congress; they were the only colony to opt out of the convention.

But once battles started erupting, the fact that America was at war could no longer be ignored. Georgia finally sent some delegates to Philadelphia in 1775, and in 1776 Walton was elected to go as well. Not considered to be as radical as fellow Georgians Lyman Hall or Button Gwinnett, Walton nonetheless performed well in Congress and would serve longer than his two signer colleagues, finally leaving in 1781 only because he felt he had to fight in the militia.

Walton looked a bit like a ponytailed Augustus Gloop, with a baby face that belied his reputed impatience with opinions that differed from his own. As evidenced by the wide range of dates given for Walton's birth, there is clearly still some confusion surrounding his birthday. If one is inclined to believe the account of signer Benjamin Rush—the self-appointed scribe for Congress—Walton, not Rutledge, was the youngest signer. Rush writes: "He was the youngest member of Congress, not being quite three and twenty when he signed the declaration of independence." So, thanks to Rush we can add 1753 to the list of birthdate candidates. But lacking additional proof, the honor of youngest signer must stay with South Carolina's Edward Rutledge.

Walton left Congress in 1778 to fight as a colonel in the militia. He was shot and fell from his horse in the siege on Savannah. His troops scattered, and Walton was immediately captured by the British. He was treated with kindness by the ranking officer, who granted him parole so he could seek private medical care for the wound in his thigh. Once he was sufficiently healed, he was rounded up and tossed in a Sunbury, Georgia, jail. It's possible that Walton, a colonel and a signer, was considered a plum prisoner, the perfect bargaining chip to exchange for a high-ranking British officer. He was held prisoner for close to a year while his captors waited for the right moment to play their hand. The British had wanted a brigadier general released in exchange for Walton, but settled for a naval captain in the end.

Another Founding Father gout sufferer, Walton was left with a limp from his war injury in addition to the excruciatingly tender, aching feet that are common with gout. Walton didn't let his pains slow him down, though. In his post-Congress life, he served as Georgia's chief justice, governor, and U.S. senator, among other judicial posts. He was also a trustee of Franklin College, which would become the University of Georgia. In 1790 he built a cottage called Meadow Garden in Augusta, but five years later moved to a country estate called College Hill on the outskirts of town. He died there in 1804 and was buried in Rosney Cemetery in Augusta. His remains were later reinterred beneath a monument in the signers' honor on the grounds of the courthouse in Augusta.

Button Gwinnett

THE SIGNER WITH THE $700,000 AUTOGRAPH

BORN: About 1735

DIED: May 19, 1777

AGE AT SIGNING: About 41

PROFESSION: Merchant, planter

BURIED: Colonial Park Cemetery, Savannah, Georgia

People always make a fuss over John Hancock's ostentatious signature. But diehard autograph collectors place a much higher value on the scrawl of a man you've probably never heard of: Button Gwinnett.

Gwinnett was one of the three signers from Georgia, and yes, that was his real first name. (The last name is pronounced Gwin-NETT.) Born in England, the son of a Welsh clergyman, he was given the last name of his godmother, Barbara Button.

We'd love to tell you about all the brave acts of derring-do that Gwinnett accomplished in the service of liberty, but there are none. For one thing, he died young, at the age of forty-two, less than a year after signing the Declaration. And for another, things just never seemed to work out for poor Gwinnett. Long before the invention of the credit card, he lived his life by slapping everything on the eighteenth-century equivalent of plastic. In England, he borrowed money to make a fresh start in the New World, but he never repaid the debt. Once in the colonies, he borrowed still more, this time to try his hand as a merchant in Charleston, South Carolina—another failed venture. So he borrowed yet again, hoping to make a go of it in Savannah, Georgia—but he failed there, too. Intrigued by the life of a plantation owner, he borrowed still more money—£3,000—and bought a tract of land that included an entire island, St. Catherine's, just off the Georgia coast. He then purchased slaves to work his vast plantation. But he grew nothing but debts, and his creditors ended up seizing the land as payment, leaving him and his family only their home.

Since Gwinnett still had family and business connections in England, he initially resisted the colonial cry to break with the king. He griped to anyone who would listen that participating in this revolutionary business would only come back to haunt him. He lived on an island, for Pete's sake! His family and home were vulnerable to British ships. Eventually he changed his mind, possibly swayed by the charismatic Lyman Hall, a fellow signer from Georgia. Gwinnett distinguished himself in politics well enough to be chosen as a delegate to the Second Continental Congress. He voted for and signed the Declaration in Philadelphia, still griping about his island, and then scurried back home to Georgia, clutching a pamphlet by John Adams that might as well have been called "How to Write Your Own State Constitution." Gwinnett proceeded to do just that for his adopted home state.

As the Revolutionary War began, Gwinnett envisioned a great future for himself as both Georgia's governor and head of Georgia's contingent of the Continental Army, but his peers thought it foolish for him to handle both positions. When the state's first governor died, they made Gwinnett acting governor and placed the guns and soldiers in the seasoned hands of a trained military man, Colonel Lachlan McIntosh. Gwinnett resented the decision and forever regarded the newly commissioned McIntosh as his sworn enemy. He accused McIntosh's brother George of treason, purged Georgia's executive council of McIntosh's allies, and went behind McIntosh's back to mount a failed military campaign to British-held Florida.

When summoned before the legislature to explain the disastrous scheme, Gwinnett sweet-talked his way out of trouble, but his colleagues wisely refused to vote him in as Georgia's official governor. General McIntosh mocked Gwinnett in front of his peers, calling him a "scoundrel and a lying rascal." The baiting worked. Seething with rage, Gwinnett challenged his nemesis to a duel. This was perfectly logical: it makes good sense for civilians to pick gunfights with army generals.

The very next day, the two met in a field east of Savannah, loaded their pistols, marched off twelve paces, and fired. Both were hit, but only Gwinnett's wound was mortal. A few days later, he died from gangrene in his festering leg. He was buried in Savannah in a spot that is today known as Colonial Park Cemetery. He was just the second signer to die. (John Morton of Pennsylvania was the first.)

At first glance, poor Gwinnett seems not to have made much of an impression on his contemporaries. His grave was poorly marked, and its location remained a mystery well into the twentieth century. Historians aren't even completely sure what he looked like, because no authenticated portraits of him have ever been found. His name has become associated with early American political pettiness and short temper.

And yet, Gwinnett's strange legacy lives on, arguably more so than that of most of his fellow signers. Georgia has a Gwinnett County, and there are banks, golf courses, streets, and even elementary schools named after him. In the rarefied world of philography (autograph collecting), Gwinnett's signature has long been regarded as one of the rarest. Only about thirty specimens exist, and many are held in museums or private collections. In 2010, a letter bearing Gwinnett's signature was auctioned by Sotheby's for the unheard-of sum of $722,500. A forged Gwinnett signature (a common occurrence, by the way) is the subject of "Button, Button," a 1953 science-fiction story by Isaac Asimov. And an old American folk saying describes something uncommon as being "as rare as a Button Gwinnett."

As for Gwinnett's final resting place, in the 1950s a history buff claimed to have found Gwinnett's grave in Savannah. The remains were exhumed and sent to the Smithsonian Institution for analysis, but the results were equivocal and contentious. Nevertheless, the city of Augusta demanded that Savannah turn over the disputed remains for Augusta's Signers Monument, a hallowed interment site for Georgia's two other Declaration signers, Lyman Hall and George Walton. Savannah refused, saying it would build its own Gwinnett memorial—just as soon as it raised the money. While the city scrounged up the cash to erect the marble structure, Gwinnett's alleged bones reposed in an oak casket in his discoverer's guest room. They were finally reburied in the original cemetery in the early 1960s, in a ceremony at which one eulogizer intoned (we kid you not): "We no longer need to ask, 'Button, Button, who has the Button?' Button has been found."

Incidentally, Gwinnett's predictions about St. Catherine's Island came true. During the Revolutionary War, British troops invaded and ransacked his home. (Historians are unclear about what happened to Gwinnett's family.) The island passed to a series of owners and today is a privately held nature habitat, largely closed to the public. An old house on the island, constructed of "tabby"—mortar fashioned from lime, seashells, and sand—is believed to be all that remains of the Gwinnett family home.

Button Gwinnett

Appendixes

Appendix I.
The Declaration of Independence

The Text of the Declaration of Independence
IN CONGRESS, JULY 4, 1776

The unanimous Declaration of the thirteen united States of America

When in the Course of human events it becomes necessary for one people to dissolve the political bands which have connected them with another and to assume among the powers of the earth, the separate and equal station to which the Laws of Nature and of Nature's God entitle them, a decent respect to the opinions of mankind requires that they should declare the causes which impel them to the separation.—

We hold these truths to be self-evident, that all men are created equal, that they are endowed by their Creator with certain unalienable Rights, that among these are Life, Liberty and the pursuit of Happiness.—

That to secure these rights, Governments are instituted among Men, deriving their just powers from the consent of the governed, —

That whenever any Form of Government becomes destructive of these ends, it is the Right of the People to alter or to abolish it, and to institute new Government, laying its foundation on such principles and organizing its powers in such form, as to them shall seem most likely to effect their Safety and Happiness. Prudence, indeed, will dictate that Governments long established should not be changed for light and transient causes; and accordingly all experience hath shewn that mankind are more disposed to suffer, while evils are sufferable than to right themselves by abolishing the forms to which they are accustomed. But when a long train of abuses and usurpations, pursuing invariably the same Object evinces a design to reduce them under absolute Despotism, it is their right, it is their duty, to throw off such Government, and to provide new Guards for their future security.—

Such has been the patient sufferance of these Colonies; and such is now the necessity which constrains them to alter their former Systems of Government. The history of the present king of Great Britain is a history of repeated injuries and usurpations, all having in direct object the establishment of an absolute Tyranny over these States. To prove this, let Facts be submitted to a candid world.—

He has refused his Assent to Laws, the most wholesome and necessary for the public good.—

He has forbidden his Governors to pass Laws of immediate and pressing importance, unless suspended in their operation till his Assent should be obtained; and when so suspended, he has utterly neglected to attend to them.—

He has refused to pass other Laws for the accommodation of large districts of people, unless those people would relinquish the right of Representation in the Legislature, a right inestimable to them and formidable to tyrants only.—

He has called together legislative bodies at places unusual, uncomfortable, and distant from the depository of their Public Records, for the sole purpose of fatiguing them into compliance with his measures.—

He has dissolved Representative Houses repeatedly, for opposing with manly firmness his invasions on the rights of the people.—

He has refused for a long time, after such dissolutions, to cause others to be elected, whereby the Legislative Powers, incapable of Annihilation, have returned to the People at large for their exercise; the State remaining in the mean time exposed to all the dangers of invasion from without, and convulsions within.—

He has endeavoured to prevent the population of these States; for that purpose obstructing the Laws for Naturalization of Foreigners; refusing to pass others to encourage their migrations hither, and raising the conditions of new Appropriations of Lands.—

He has obstructed the Administration of Justice by refusing his Assent to Laws for establishing Judiciary Powers.—

He has made Judges dependent on his Will alone for the tenure of their offices, and the amount and payment of their salaries.—

He has erected a multitude of New Offices, and sent hither swarms of Officers to harrass our people and eat out their substance.—

He has kept among us, in times of peace, Standing Armies without the Consent of our legislatures.—

He has affected to render the Military independent of and superior to the Civil Power.—

He has combined with others to subject us to a jurisdiction foreign to our constitution, and unacknowledged by our laws; giving his Assent to their Acts of pretended Legislation:—

For quartering large bodies of armed troops among us:—

For protecting them, by a mock Trial from punishment for any Murders which they should commit on the Inhabitants of these States:—

For cutting off our Trade with all parts of the world:

For imposing Taxes on us without our Consent:—

For depriving us in many cases, of the benefit of Trial by Jury:

For transporting us beyond Seas to be tried for pretended offences:—

For abolishing the free System of English Laws in a neighbouring Province, establishing therein an Arbitrary government, and enlarging its Boundaries so as to render it at once an example and fit instrument for introducing the same absolute rule into these Colonies:—

For taking away our Charters, abolishing our most valuable Laws and altering fundamentally the Forms of our Governments:—

For suspending our own Legislatures, and declaring themselves invested with power to legislate for us in all cases whatsoever.—

He has abdicated Government here, by declaring us out of his Protection and waging War against us.—

He has plundered our seas, ravaged our coasts, burnt our towns, and destroyed the lives of our people.—

He is at this time transporting large Armies of foreign Mercenaries to compleat the works of death, desolation, and tyranny, already begun with circumstances of Cruelty & Perfidy scarcely paralleled in the most barbarous ages, and totally unworthy the Head of a civilized nation.—

He has constrained our fellow Citizens taken Captive on the high Seas to bear Arms against their Country, to become the executioners of their friends and Brethren, or to fall themselves by their Hands.—

He has excited domestic insurrections amongst us, and has endeavoured to bring on the inhabitants of our frontiers, the merciless Indian Savages whose known rule of warfare, is an undistinguished destruction of all ages, sexes and conditions.

In every stage of these Oppressions We have Petitioned for Redress in the most humble terms: Our repeated Petitions have been answered only by repeated injury. A Prince, whose character is thus marked by every act which may define a Tyrant, is unfit to be the ruler of a free people.

Nor have We been wanting in attentions to our British brethren. We have warned them from time to time of attempts by their legislature to extend an unwarrantable jurisdiction over us. We have reminded them of the circumstances of our emigration and settlement here. We have appealed to their native justice and magnanimity, and we have conjured them by the ties of our common kindred to disavow these usurpations, which would inevitably interrupt our connections and correspondence. They too have been deaf to the voice of justice and of consanguinity. We must, therefore, acquiesce in the necessity, which denounces our Separation, and hold them, as we hold the rest of mankind, Enemies in War, in Peace Friends.—

We, therefore, the Representatives of the united States of America, in General Congress, Assembled, appealing to the Supreme Judge of the world for the rectitude of our intentions, do, in the Name, and by Authority of the good People of these Colonies, solemnly publish and declare, That these united Colonies are, and of Right ought to be Free and Independent States, that they are Absolved from all Allegiance to the British Crown, and that all political connection between them and the State of Great Britain, is and ought to be totally dissolved; and that as Free and Independent States, they have full Power to levy War, conclude Peace, contract Alliances, establish Commerce, and to do all other Acts and Things which Independent States may of right do.—

And for the support of this Declaration, with a firm reliance on the protection of Divine Providence, we mutually pledge to each other our Lives, our Fortunes, and our sacred Honor.

Timeline

Here are some key milestones in the saga of the Declaration of Independence.

1763 The French and Indian Wars, a series of conflicts between Great Britain and France, in which many of the signers and their ancestors fought, end in treaty.

1765 The Stamp Act, requiring tax be paid on all printed papers—from official documents to playing cards—passes, infuriating many colonists.

1770 The Boston Massacre

1773 The Boston Tea Party

1774 March: British Parliament passes several laws, which they called the Coercive Acts. The colonists refer to them as the Intolerable Acts. Among others, these included the Boston Port Act, which closed the port of Boston, and the Quartering Act, which demanded colonists house British soldiers whenever deemed necessary.

September: First Continental Congress convenes. Later this year, the Articles of Association are signed, in which the colonies agree to a nonimportation, nonconsumption, and nonexportation stance with the British.

1775 April: Paul Revere rides, and the battles of Lexington and Concord start the Revolutionary War.

May: The Second Continental Congress meets.

June: George Washington is made commander in chief of the Continental Army.

1776 June 7: Richard Henry Lee of Virginia proposes separation from Great Britain. Congress postpones vote on his resolution for a month. The Committee of Five is formed to write the Declaration of Independence.

July 1: "Informal" vote on independence.

July 2: Vote to separate from Great Britain passes in Congress.

July 4: The Declaration of Independence is adopted. Dunlap Broadsides are printed that night to be distributed throughout the colonies.

July 9: New York, the only colony to abstain from the vote on July 2, assents to break with Great Britain.

July 19: Engrossed Declaration of Independence is ordered.

August 2: The majority of signers affix their names to the engrossed Declaration of Independence.

December: Washington crosses the Delaware and gives the colonies their first major win at Trenton.

1777 Articles of Confederation, a "pre-Constitution" that governed the states in the first years after the Declaration of Independence, are signed.

1781 Cornwallis surrenders at Yorktown.

1783 The Treaty of Paris is signed. The war is over.

1787 On September 17, 1787, the Constitution is adopted. In December, Delaware becomes the first state to ratify the document.

1788 New Hampshire becomes the ninth state to ratify the Constitution, putting the historic document into effect.

1789 George Washington takes office as the first president of the United States under the new Constitution.

Appendix II.
The Miscellany of Independence

Here's an assortment of strange trivia regarding the Declaration of Independence. What's really on the back of this legendary document? Who deserves credit for the fancy handwriting? How did King George III react? And was there really a fifty-seventh signer? Read on.

So What's Really Written on the Back?

The 2004 film *National Treasure* suggested that clues to buried treasure were hidden on the reverse of the Declaration of Independence. The movie was enormously popular, and it's led many people to wonder what, if anything, is really written on the back. Here is the answer (sorry, folks, no clues or secret messages): "Original Declaration of Independence dated 4th July 1776."

As anticlimactic as this text may seem, it had a purpose. The Declaration made a lot of rounds during its early life, often in the satchel of a courier and in the company of a number of other important documents that needed safeguarding. It would have been very time-consuming to unroll each and every scroll in the sack to find the really important ones, so the document was identified on the back, which then became the front when it was rolled up all neat and tidy.

Preserving Independence

In the 176 years following its signing, the Declaration was stored in several unlikely locations—everywhere from an abandoned gristmill to private homes to Fort Knox. Finally, in 1952, the document landed in the National Archives, in Washington, D.C., where archivists attempted to preserve it with the best known technology. This meant that for the next fifty years, it was stored in a glass case filled with helium. But by 2001, the case was deteriorating, and so it was completely redesigned.

The new titanium-frame casing has a touch of gold plating and is fitted with a laminated, antireflective pane—which never touches the document—composed of polyvinyl butyral sandwiched between two panes of glass. This combination is designed to withstand bombs, bullets, hurricanes, and other disasters, natural or otherwise. Perhaps most important, it also blocks damaging ultraviolet rays. The temperature inside the super-case is kept at around 67°F (19°C), and the atmosphere inside does not contain oxygen, but rather humidified argon. (The Declaration needs just a touch of humidity, around 45 percent, to keep it from becoming too brittle.)

In addition, the new case can be opened and resealed without damaging the Declaration's integrity. The same technology is being used to preserve the other Charters of Freedom, the U.S. Constitution and the Bill of Rights.

Über-Signers

Once some people get a taste for signing, they just can't stop. Here are some signers who affixed their name to more than one of America's most historic documents.

Sixteen who signed both the Declaration of Independence and the Articles of Confederation: Josiah Bartlett, John Hancock, Samuel Adams, Elbridge Gerry, William Ellery, Roger Sherman, Samuel Huntington, Oliver Wolcott, Francis Lewis, John Witherspoon, Robert Morris, Thomas McKean, Richard Henry Lee, Francis Lightfoot Lee, John Penn, and Thomas Heyward Jr.

Six who signed both the Declaration of Independence & the U.S. Constitution: Roger Sherman, Benjamin Franklin, Robert Morris, George Clymer, James Wilson, and George Read

Two who signed the Declaration of Independence, the Articles of Confederation, and the U.S. Constitution (aka "The Big Three"): Robert Morris and Roger Sherman

And finally, the Top Über-Signer, the only man to have signed the Articles of Association, the Declaration of Independence, the Articles of Confederation, and the U.S. Constitution: Roger Sherman

The Penman of Congress

On August 2, 1776, the majority of the signers affixed their names to what is known as the engrossed document. Today this version of the Declaration of Independence is kept in the National Archives under a few inches of very thick, bulletproof glass. "Engrossed" is a fancy way of saying that it was a nice piece of parchment with some very loopy lettering. The man whom historians consider most likely to have put feathered quill to parchment to create this little piece of calligraphic history was Timothy Matlack.

On July 19, 1776, the word came down from Congress that the new Declaration should be "fairly engrossed on parchment, with the title and stile of 'The unanimous declaration of the thirteen United States of America,' and that the same, when engrossed, be signed by every member of Congress."

Well, now. A quick look at the second line of the engrossed document tells us that Matlack went a little off the board when following Congress's style mandate. Although "States" is capitalized, "united" is not. In fact, "united" is squeezed in there like ten pounds of sausage stuffed into a five-pound sack. Maybe Matlack ran into the same bind encountered by every kid making a birthday card for parents: he started out big and fancy and then realized there wasn't enough space for all the words.

In a sense, his mistake—if it was one—was a representation of the sentiment of the times. The colonies wanted to be united, especially for their defense, but many citizens were still strongly in favor of their own sovereignty and not quite sure how they felt about another big government. And so the Federalist-Republican battle began. Even today, the question of states' rights versus federal rights remains a sticky subject. Taking the emphasis off "united" may have been subconscious; a subliminal message to readers that said, "Yes, we're united, but we still have a few kinks to work out in the self-governing arena." Cut to the Civil War . . .

Matlack is also credited as scrivener of George Washington's commission as commanding general of the Continental Army. The scribe was a radical, a brewer, and the founder of the Society for Free Quakers, an organization for folks who had been given the boot by the Friends for the bellicose stance they took during the Revolutionary War. In fact, after two Quakers criticized his sons for taking up arms in the conflict, Matlack had them caned. People openly mocked him for wearing his sword around town. But apparently, Matlack, of all people, did not subscribe to the belief that the pen was mightier than the sword (or the cane, for that matter).

The Almost-Presidents

Some historians consider four signers to be among the "unofficial" presidents of the United States who served before George Washington took office. Their official title was "President of the United States in Congress Assembled." These men presided over Congress after the adoption of the Articles of Confederation, the first document proclaiming that the thirteen sovereign states that had declared independence from Great Britain would begin to work together as one nation.

Following is the complete list of Presidents of the United States in Congress Assembled and the years they served:

Signer Samuel Huntington of Connecticut, 1781
Signer Thomas McKean of Delaware, 1781
John Hanson of Maryland, 1781–82
Elias Boudinot of New Jersey, 1782–83
Thomas Mifflin of Pennsylvania, 1783–84
Signer Richard Henry Lee of Virginia, 1784–85
Signer John Hancock of Massachusetts, 1785–86
Nathaniel Gorham of Massachusetts, 1786
Arthur St. Clair of Pennsylvania, 1787
Cyrus Griffin of Virginia, 1788–89

And then finally, presiding over the nation under the Constitution of the United States . . .

George Washington of Virginia, president of the United States, 1789–97

Dunlap and His Broadsides

After the Declaration of Independence was accepted by Congress and signed by Hancock and his secretary, Charles Thomson, the delegates wanted to get the word out that the big break with Great Britain was official. Congress immediately printed two hundred copies and sent them all over the colonies—to George Washington and his troops, to newspapers, to anyone who would read the document or pass it on. Who made these printed copies? Congress's official pressman, John Dunlap.

Dunlap, a Philadelphia printer, worked his little typesetting fingers to the bone on the night of July 4 so that copies would be ready the next day. The broadside looks markedly different from the Declaration of Independence that we're used to seeing. Instead of fancy-schmancy handwritten script, it has typeset print. The only names on the document belong to John Hancock and Charles Thomson, secretary of Congress, and these are typeset as well. And the title referred to the document as merely "a declaration," since New York had not yet assented to the separation. When it did, on July 9, the title of the engrossed document and future copies were changed to "a unanimous declaration." Washington got his copy and had it read to his troops on July 9 to get them all fired up (and perhaps take their minds off their lack of shoes and food).

Today, twenty-five Dunlap broadsides are known; twenty are owned by American institutions, two are in British institutions, and three are held by some very lucky private owners. The whereabouts of the other 175 copies are unknown. So you never know where they might turn up. In 1989, a man perusing a flea market bought a $4 frame and took his prize home. The enclosed painting was torn, and as he fiddled with it, he discovered a Dunlap broadside tucked inside. It was evaluated, identified as one of the originals, and in 2000 was sold at a live Sotheby's Internet auction for $8.14 million to television producer Norman Lear and associates.

All in the Family

Considering that only about 2.5 million people lived in the colonies at the time of independence, it's not surprising that more than a few of them were related to one another. And when you narrow that population to the select group of families with means and political influence, you'll quickly discover that more than a few signers were connected through blood or marriage.

The Lee brothers of Virginia, Richard Henry and Francis Lightfoot, are the only immediate relations who signed the Declaration of Independence. They were almost joined by Thomas Lynch Jr. of South Carolina, whose father was a Congressman at the time. But, due to illness, Lynch Sr. could not vote or sign. Massachusetts rebels John Adams and Samuel Adams were signing cousins, as were Carter Braxton, Benjamin Harrison, and Thomas Nelson Jr. of Virginia.

Signer George Ross of Pennsylvania was not only the uncle of revolutionary seamstress Betsy Ross, he was also brother-in-law to Delaware's George Read. Arthur Middleton and Edward Rutledge of South Carolina were brothers-in-law. Signer Benjamin Rush of Pennsylvania married Julia, the daughter of New Jersey signer Richard Stockton, and their marriage was presided over by another New Jersey signer, John Witherspoon.

No wonder they gave birth to a new nation—they were all in a family way . . .

The Madness of King George

Needless to say, England was less than thrilled with the decision of her prized colonies to split from the fold. Here are some remarks from King George III spoken to Parliament on October 31, 1776:

"Nothing could have afforded me so much satisfaction as to have been able to inform you at the opening of this session, that the troubles, which have so long distracted my colonies in North America, were at an end; and that my unhappy people, recovered from their delusion, had delivered themselves from the oppression of their leaders and returned to their duty. But so daring and desperate is the spirit of those leaders, whose object has always been dominion and power, that they have now openly renounced all allegiance to the Crown, and all political connection with this country: They have rejected, with circumstances of indignity and insult, the means of conciliation held out to them under the authority of our commission; and have presumed to set up their rebellious confederacies for independent states. If their treason be suffered to take root, much mischief must grow from it, to the safety of my loyal colonies, to the commerce of my kingdoms, and indeed to the present system of all Europe. One great advantage, however, will be derived from the object of the rebels being openly avowed, and clearly understood; we shall have unanimity at home, founded in the general conviction of the justice and necessity of our measures."

Immigrant Signers

Not all of the Founding Fathers began their lives in the colonies. Those signers born outside the original thirteen states are:

Button Gwinnett of Georgia
Born Gloucester, England, c. 1735

Francis Lewis of New York
Born Llandaff, Wales, 1713

Robert Morris of Pennsylvania
Born Lancashire, England, 1734

James Smith of Pennsylvania
Born Ireland, c. 1719

George Taylor of Pennsylvania
Born Ireland, c. 1716

Matthew Thornton of New Hampshire
Born Ireland, c. 1714

James Wilson of Pennsylvania
Born Carskerdo, Scotland, 1742

John Witherspoon of New Jersey
Born Gifford, Scotland, 1723

Charles Thomson, the Fifty-Seventh Signer

Only two people signed the Declaration of Independence on July 4. The first was president of Congress John Hancock. The only other person to sign the originally adopted, first-ever copy of the Declaration of Independence on July 4, 1776, was Charles Thomson. In fact, the first printed broadsides distributed throughout the colonies bore only the names of these two men.

So who was this man, whom some historians call the fifty-seventh signer, the man John Adams referred to as "the Samuel Adams of Philadelphia, the life of the cause of liberty"? A Philadelphia merchant (and amateur distiller of rum), Thomson was secretary of Congress for fifteen years, through both the First and Second Continental Congresses and into the Confederation Congress as well. Delegates may have come and gone, but Charles Thomson remained.

Besides keeping track of all Congress's pertinent correspondence and record of their actions and votes, Thomson is credited with assembling the final design of the Great Seal of the United States.

Three prior committees had tried their best to come up with an appropriate emblem for the new country, but it was Thomson who combined elements from those attempts into the design still visible today on the back of the dollar bill.

One of Thomson's final duties was to travel to Mount Vernon to notify George Washington that he had been elected as first president of the United States. Thomson rode back with the incumbent, attended the inauguration, and tendered his resignation later that year. He spent the remainder of his days writing scholarly books and translating the bible from Greek into English.

Selected Bibliography

Adams, John. *The Diary and Autobiography of John Adams*. Vol. 2, *Diary 1771–1781*. L. H. Butterfield, ed. Cambridge: Belknap Press of Harvard University Press, 1962.

————. *The Works of John Adams, Second President of the United States, With a Life of the Author*. Vol. 8. Charles Francis Adams, ed. Boston: Little, Brown, 1853.

Bakeless, John, and Katherine Bakeless. *Signers of the Declaration of Independence*. Boston: Houghton-Mifflin, 1969.

Barber, John W., and Henry Howe. *Historical Collections of the State of New Jersey*. New York: S. Tuttle, 1844.

Baxter, Katherine Schuyler. *A Godchild of Washington: A Picture of the Past*. New York: F. Tennyson Neely, 1897.

Bicknell, Thomas Williams. *The History of the State of Rhode Island and Providence Plantations*. Vol. 2. New York: The American Historical Society, 1920.

Biddle, Louis Alexander, ed. *A Memorial Containing Travels Through Life; or Sundry Incidents in the Life of Benjamin Rush*. Philadelphia: Private family printing, 1905.

Boutell, Lewis Henry. *The Life of Roger Sherman*. Chicago: A.C. McClurg, 1896.

Brodsky, Alyn. *Benjamin Rush: Patriot and Physician*. New York: Truman Talley Books, 2004.

Channing, William Ellery. *Memoir of William Ellery Channing with Extracts from His Correspondence and Manuscripts*, Vol. 1. Adamant Media Corp., 2001.

Chernow, Barbara Ann. *Robert Morris: Land Speculator, 1790–1801*. New York: Columbia University Press, 1974.

Clark, J. Henry. *The Medical Men of New Jersey, in Essex District, from 1666 to 1866*. Newark: Private printing, Evening Courier Office, 1867.

Cook, James F. *The Governors of Georgia, 1754–2004*. Macon, Ga.: Mercer University Press, 2004.

Ellis, John Tracy. *American Catholicism*. 2d rev. ed. Chicago: University of Chicago Press, 1969.

Fehrenbach, T. R. *Greatness to Spare: The Heroic Sacrifices of the Men Who Signed the Declaration of Independence*. Bridgewater, N.J.: Replica Books (reprint), 1999.

Ferris, Robert G., and Richard E. Morris. *The Signers of the Declaration of Independence*. National Park Service, 1973; Arlington, Va.: Interpretive Publications, 1982.

Fox-Genovese, Elizabeth, and Eugene D. Genovese. *The Mind of the Master Class: History and Faith in the Southern Slaveholders' Worldview*. Cambridge, Eng.: Cambridge University Press, 2005.

Fowler, William F. *William Ellery: A Rhode Island Politico and Lord of the Admiralty*. Metuchen, N.J.: Scarecrow Press, 1973.

Fradin, Dennis Brindell. *The Signers: The 56 Stories Behind the Declaration of Independence*. New York: Walker & Company, 2002.

Goodrich, Charles Augustus. *Our Lives, Our Fortunes and Our Sacred Honor: The Lives of the Signers to the Declaration of Independence*. New York: William Reed & Co., 1856 (accessed via colonialhall.com).

Green, Harry Clinton, and Mary Wolcott Green. *The Pioneer Mothers of America: A Record of the More Notable Women of the Early Days of the Country, and Particularly of the Colonial and Revolutionary Periods*. Vol.3. New York: G.P. Putnam's Sons, 1912.

Hansard, Thomas Curson. *The Parliamentary History of England from the Earliest Period to the Year 1803*. London: T. C. Hansard et al., 1813.

Hart, Charles Henry. *Robert Morris, the Financier of the American Revolution: A Sketch*. Philadelphia: Collins, Printer, 1877.

Haw, James. *John & Edward Rutledge of South Carolina*. Athens: University of Georgia Press, 1997.

Hazelton, John Hampden. *The Declaration of Independence: Its History*. New York: Dodd, Mead & Co., 1906.

Higginson, Thomas Wentworth. *Travellers and Outlaws: Episodes in American History*. Boston: Lee and Shepard, 1889.

The Historical Society of Pennsylvania. *The Pennsylvania Magazine of History and Biography*. Vol. 1. Philadelphia: Pennsylvania Historical Periodicals, 1877.

Isaacson, Walter. *Benjamin Franklin: An American Life*. New York: Simon & Schuster, 2003.

Jefferson, Thomas. *Virginia Reports, Jefferson—33 Grattan: Reports of Cases Determined in the General Court of Virginia, from 1730 to 1740; and from 1768 to 1772.*

Thomas Johnson Michie, ed. Charlottesville, Va.: The Michie Co., 1903.

———. *The Writings of Thomas Jefferson*. Andrew A. Lipscomb, et al., eds. Washington, D.C.: The Thomas Jefferson Memorial Association, 1905.

Kelly, M. Ruth. *The Olmsted Case: Privateers, Property, and Politics in Pennsylvania, 1778–1810*. Selinsgrove, Pa.: Susquehanna University Press, 2005.

Laird, Archibald. *Profitable Company: Milestones and Monuments of the Signers of the Declaration of Independence*. Norwell, Mass.: The Christopher Publishing House, 1987.

Lamb, Martha J., ed. *The Magazine of American History with Notes and Queries*, Vol. 25, *January–June, 1891*. New York: Historical Publication Co., 1891.

Laurens, Henry. *The Papers of Henry Laurens*. Vol. 9. Columbia: University of South Carolina Press, 1981.

Lincoln, Robert W. *Lives of the Presidents of the United States: With Biographical Notices of the Signers of the Declaration of Independence*. New York: N. Watson & Co., 1836.

Lossing, Benson J. *Lives of the Signers of the Declaration of Independence*. New York: Cooledge & Brother, 1848. Reprint, Aledo, Tex.: WallBuilder Press, 1995.

Maine Historical Society. *Collections and Proceedings of the Maine Historical Society*. Second Series, Vol. 6. Portland: Maine Historical Society, 1895.

Malone, Dumas. *The Story of the Declaration of Independence*. New York: Oxford University Press, 1954.

McCullough, David. *1776*. New York: Simon & Schuster, 2005.

McDonough, Daniel J. *Christopher Gadsden and Henry Laurens: The Parallel Lives of Two American Patriots*. Selinsgrove, Pa.: Susquehanna University Press, 2000.

Melish, Joanne Pope. *Disowning Slavery: Gradual Emancipation and "Race" in New England, 1780–1860*. Ithaca, N.Y.: Cornell University Press, 1998.

Meyers, Donald J. *And the War Came: The Slavery Quarrel and the American Civil War*. New York: Algora Publishing, 2005.

Miller, Marion Mills. *American Debate: A History of Political and Economic Controversy in the United States, With Critical Digests of Leading Debates*. G.P. Putnam's Sons, 1916.

Mitchell, Memory F. *North Carolina's Signers: Brief Sketches of the Men Who Signed the Declaration of Independence and the Constitution*. Raleigh, N.C.: Raleigh State Department of Archives and History, 1964.

Morris, Anne Cary, ed. *The Diary and Letters of Gouverneur Morris: Minister of the United States to France; Member of the Constitutional Convention, etc*. Vol. 2. New York: Charles Scribner's Sons, 1888.

Morris, Robert. *The Confidential Correspondence of Robert Morris, the Great Financier of the Revolution*. Reprint, Whitefish, Mt.: Kessinger Publishing, 2005.

Mulford, Carla, ed. *Only for the Eye of a Friend: The Poems of Annis Boudinot Stockton*. Charlottesville: University of Virginia Press, 1995.

Oberholtzer, Ellis Paxton. *Robert Morris: Patriot and Financier*. New York: Macmillan Company, 1903. Reprint, New York: B. Franklin, 1968.

Osgood, Herbert I., et al., eds. *Minutes of the Common Council of the City of New York, 1675–1776*. New York: Dodd, Mead and Company, 1905.

Papas, Phillip. *That Ever Loyal Island: Staten Island and the American Revolution*. New York: New York University Press, 2007.

Pearson, Michael. *Those Damned Rebels: The American Revolution as Seen Through British Eyes*. New York: G.P. Putnam's Sons, 1972.

Publishing Society of New York, Americana Society. *The American Historical Magazine*. New York: The Publishing Society of New York, 1906.

Quinn, Bro. C. Edward, FSC. *Signers of the Declaration of Independence*. New York: The Bronx County Historical Society, 1987.

Randall, Willard Sterne. *Thomas Jefferson: A Life*. New York: HarperCollins, 1994.

Raphael, Ray. *Founding Myths: Stories That Hide Our Patriotic Past*. New York: New Press, 2004.

Ratzlaff, Robert K. *John Rutledge Jr.: South Carolina Federalist, 1766–1819*. New York: Arno Press, 1982.

Read, William Thompson. *Life and Correspondence of George Read: A Signer of the Declaration of Independence*. Philadelphia: J. B. Lippincott & Co., 1870.

Ripley, George, and Charles A. Dana. *The New American Cyclopaedia: A Popular Dictionary of General Knowledge*. Vol. 9. New York: D. Appleton & Company, 1860.

Rush, Benjamin. *Essay, Literary, Moral and Philosophical*. Philadelphia: Thomas and William Bradford, 1806.

Sanderson, John. *Biography of the Signers of the Declaration of Independence*. Vol. 1. Philadelphia: R. W. Pomeroy, 1820; Reprint, Kessinger Publishing, 2008.

Sanderson, John, Robert Waln, and Henry D. Gilpin, eds. *Biography of the Signers of the Declaration of Independence*. Vols. 1–9. Philadelphia: R. W. Pomeroy, 1820–1827.

Scheer, George F., and Hugh F. Rankin. *Rebels & Redcoats: The American Revolution Through the Eyes of Those Who Fought and Lived It*. Cambridge, Mass.: Da Capo Press, 1987.

Serle, Ambrose. *The American Journal of Ambrose Serle, Secretary to Lord Howe, 1776–1778*. Edward H. Tatum Jr., ed. New York: The New York Times and Arno Press, 1969.

Sinclair, Merle, and Annabel Douglas McArthur. *They Signed for Us*. New York: Duell, Sloan and Pearce, 1957.

Snowden, Yates, and Harry Gardner Cutler, eds. *History of South Carolina*. Vol. 1. Chicago: Lewis Publishing Company, 1920.

South, Stanley A. *An Archaeological Evolution*. New York: Springer, 2005.

South Carolina Historical Society. *South Carolina Historical and Genealogical Magazine*. Vol. 2, no. 2. Charleston: The Walker, Evans and Cogswell Co., 1900.

Stevens, J. A., et al., eds. *The Magazine of American History with Notes and Queries,*. Vol. 7. New York: A. S. Barnes and Co., 1881.

Stone, Peter, and Sherman Edwards. *1776: A Musical Play*. New York: Viking Press, 1970.

Sumner, William Graham. *Robert Morris*. New York: Dodd, Mead and Co., 1892.

Sweet, John Wood. *Bodies Politic: Negotiating Race in the American North, 1730–1830*. Baltimore: Johns Hopkins University Press, 2003.

Taylor, John M. *History in Your Hand: Fifty Years of the Manuscript Society*. Westport, Conn.: Greenwood Publishing Group, 1997.

Thomas, Evan. *John Paul Jones: Sailor, Hero, Father of the Navy*. New York: Simon and Schuster, 2004.

Thomas, Isaiah. *The History of Printing in America*. Vol. 1. Albany, N.Y.: Joel Munsell, 1874.

Tompkins, Daniel Augustus. *History of Mecklenburg County and the City of Charlotte from 1740 to 1903*. Charlotte, N.C.: Observer Printing House, 1903.

Ultan, Lloyd, and Gary Hermlyn. *The Birth of the Bronx, 1609–1900*. New York: The Bronx County Historical Society, 2000.

Van Noppen, Leonard Charles, ed. *Biographical History of North Carolina from Colonial Times to the Present*. Vol. 3. Greensboro, N.C.: Charles L. Van Noppen, 1906.

Witherspoon, John. *Treatises on Justification and Regeneration*. Amherst, Mass.: J. S. & C. Adams and Co., 1830.

———. *The Works of John Witherspoon*. Vol. 2. Philadelphia: William W. Woodward, 1802.

Additional Resources & Websites

The Albert and Shirley Small Special Collections Library, University of Virginia Library.

Brown University Steering Committee on Slavery and Justice, Brown University Library, Center for Digital Initiatives.

The Library of Congress

The National Archives

Monticello Plantation Database, monticello.org

Index

Acknowledgments

Although it did not take a congress of men in powdered wigs to edit and create this book, we nevertheless incurred a few debts along the way. The largest is to due to Jason Rekulak, our editor, whose patience, thoughtfulness, and generosity made this a better book. Copy editor Mary Ellen Wilson also deserves thanks for helping us sharpen the manuscript. We owe a debt to Quirk designer Bryn Ashburn, who compiled disparate elements of eighteenth-century ephemera into a coherent, beautiful volume and keepsake. We thank Aurora Parlagreco for her thoughtful and sprightly redesign for the paperback edition. Lastly, thank yous all around to our family, friends, and colleagues who patiently endured tales of the signers as this book came to fruition.